Dance Makers Portfolio

conservation .... hers

....tterworth
and Gill Clarke

ISBN 1900-85-7200

First published in 1998 by the Centre for Dance and Theatre Studies
at Bretton Hall

Designed, typeset & produced by SHOUT Communications 0113 255 8570

CONTRIBUTORS

CHOREOGRAPHERS

Peter Badejo

Peter Badejo is one of Nigeria's foremost choreographers, dancers and African performance specialists, choreographer, performer, teacher and academic. His commitment to the field of African performance arts has also involved research conducted through the Universities of London, California, Ghana and Ahmadu Bello University, in addition to his own productions of allegorical contemporary African dance, including *Sisi Agbe Aye* (Opening the Gourd of Life), *The Living Circle* and **Ebo Iye** (Transitions).

Dance companies throughout Africa, Europe and America have commissioned Peter Badejo's work, and in this country he has been commissioned by companies such as Adzido, Kokuma, Irie and Sakoba. He has conducted residencies and workshop programmes throughout the UK for organisations such as the International Workshop Festival, London Contemporary Dance School, The Birmingham Summer School and his well-known annual dance and music summer school, Bami Jo. Peter Badejo has also assisted in the development of African dance in Liverpool in his work as artist in residence at Merseyside Dance Initiative.

David Bintley

Born in Huddersfield, David Bintley joined Sadler's Wells Royal Ballet in 1976. In 1978 he created his first professional work for the company, *The Outsider*. His many ballets for both Royal Ballet companies include: Consort Lessons, *Still Life at the Penguin Cafe*, *Hobson's Choice* and *Tombeaux*. As a dancer he was awarded the 1984 Laurence Olivier Award for Dance.

David Bintley was appointed Company Choreographer to Sadler's Wells Royal Ballet in 1983 and in 1986 transferred to The Royal Ballet and was Resident Choreographer until 1993. He succeeded Sir Peter Wright as Director of Birmingham Royal Ballet in 1995 and since then has created for the company, *Carmina Burana*, *The Nutcracker Sweeties* and the full length ballet, *Far from the Madding Crowd*. His ballets are in the repertory of companies in America, Canada, Germany and South Africa.

Christopher Bruce

Since 1994 Rambert Dance Company's Artistic Director, Christopher Bruce has been one of Britain's leading choreographers with an international reputation. His career developed with Rambert where he was a leading dancer and he created his earliest ballets. He has also built up special relationships with Nederlands Dans Theater, Royal Danish Ballet, Cullberg Ballet, English National Ballet (where he was Associate Choreographer 1986-1991), the Grand Theatre de Geneve and Houston Ballet (where he has been Resident Choreographer since 1989). In 1993 he received the International Theatre Institute's Award for Excellence in International Dance, and has been awarded two Evening Standard Awards for Outstanding Achievement in Ballet. In 1998 he was awarded a CBE.

Jonathan Burrows

Jonathan Burrows was born in 1960 in County Durham, England. He studied at the Royal Ballet School and was a member of The Royal Ballet from 1979 to 1991, during which time he was also choreographing. He formed his own group in 1988, and has since created seven full-length pieces for them. Although the Jonathan Burrows Group is based in London, the company are also associated with the Kunstencentrum Vooruit in Ghent, Belgium, and perform extensively internationally. In 1997 he made *Walking/music* for Ballett Frankfurt.

Siobhan Davies

Siobhan Davies was one of the first students at London Contemporary Dance School and went on to be a leading dancer and choreographer for London Contemporary Dance Theatre. In 1982, with Richard Alston and Ian Spink, she founded Second Stride and from 1988 to 1993 she was Associate Choreographer for Rambert Dance Company. She founded Siobhan Davies Dance Company in 1988. Siobhan Davies has received numerous awards including a Fulbright Arts Fellowship, four Digital Dance Awards, and five nominations for the Prudential Award for Dance which she won in 1996. Davies has been appointed both Choreographer in Residence and Senior Research Fellow at the Roehampton Institute, London and in October 1996, she accepted an Honorary Fellowship at Trinity College of Music in recognition for her creative work with music. In June 1995 she was awarded an MBE.

Stuart Hopps

Stuart Hopps was Associate Director of Scottish Ballet (1971-76). His work includes *Animal, Candide* (Edinburgh); *Pal Joey, Rocky Horror Show* (West End); *The Oresteia, Animal Farm* (RNT); *Julius Ceasar, Henry VIII, As You Like It* (RSC); and most recently the choreography and musical staging for *The Betrayal of Nora Blake* (Jermyn Street Theatre); *Border Wars* (Channel 4 TV); *Verdi's Macbeth* (The Met); *HMS Pinafore, Merry Widow* (Sadlers Wells); *Orfeo e Euridice* (Glyndebourne); *Die Fledermaus* (Scottish Opera); *Yeoman of the Guard* (D'Oyly Carte); *Christmas Eve, Cunning Little Vixen* (ENO); *HMS Pinafore* (New York); *Medea* (Barcelona); *Carmen Jones* (Old Vic); *Carmen* (ROH, Los Angeles, Seville, Barcelona); *Carmen, Idomeneo* (WNO); *Cunning Little Vixen* (Kennedy Center, ROH); and his film work includes *Much Ado About Nothing, Frankenstein, Carrington, Othello, Wings of a Dove, Hamlet* and *Amy Foster.* He is currently working on *The Passion.*

Shobana Jeyasingh

Shobana Jeyasingh has directed the Shobana Jeyasingh Dance Company since 1989. The Company has been awarded 3 Digital Dance Awards and the prestigious Prudential Award for the Arts. Jeyasingh's work for the theatre includes *Cyrano* (Royal National Theatre) and for television includes *Duets with Automobiles* for BBC2 which was shortlisted for the IMZ Dance Screen Award and *Inbetween* - a BBC2 documentary featuring the Company. In 1996 *Palimpsest* was awarded the Time Out dance award for best choreography. In 1995 Shobana Jeyasingh was awarded an MBE, an Honorary Doctorate from De Montfort University and an Honorary Masters degree from the University of Surrey.

Rosemary Lee

Rosemary Lee is a choreographer who has worked in a wide variety of contexts. In the late 80's she was known for her massive site specific projects with huge casts of all ages whilst more recently she has concentrated on solo work for theatre settings. *Charged*, an evening of her work with the Balanescu Quartet was presented at QEH last year. She has also made two dance films *boy* and *greenman* for BBC2 with film maker Peter Anderson. She collaborates regularly with visual artists, theatre directors, designers and composers. Recent commissions include *Treading the Night Plain* for Ricochet Dance Company and 3 Studies in Courtship for Transitions 1998 season.

Wayne McGregor

Wayne McGregor graduated in Dance from Bretton Hall in 1991. He created Random Dance Company in 1992, and has toured extensively with the company nationally and internationally. In September 1997 he premiered *The Millenarium* at London's South Bank. He has also choreographed for English National Opera, Shobana Jeyasingh Dance Company and Ricochet Dance Company. In 1996 he was nominated for an Olivier award in the category of Best Choreographer for the Royal National Theatre production of *A Little Night Music*. He is presently working at the National on Sean Matthias' production of *Antony and Cleopatra*.

McGregor was a recipient of the Arts Foundation Fellowship in 1994, the Lisa Ullmann travel scholarship for research into dance and technology in Japan in 1997 and the 1998 Prix d'auteur du conseil géneral de Seine-Saint-Denis. With Random he represented Britain in Bancs d"Essai Internationaux in 1998.

Lloyd Newson

Lloyd Newson studied psychology at the University of Melbourne where he started his dancing career. He received a scholarship to the London School of Contemporary Dance for two years before joining Extemporary Dance Theatre. His own company DV8 was formed in 1986, and has toured extensively, both nationally and internationally. Works reworked and filmed include *Dead Dreams of Monochrome Men, Strange Fish* and *Enter Achilles*.

Awards include the Prudential Award (twice), the Prix Italia (twice), the San Francisco International Film Festival Golden Spire award, an International Emmy for Performing Arts in 1997 and the Jury Prize of the Montreal Festival in 1998.

INTERVIEWERS

Jo Butterworth

Jo Butterworth is Head of the Centre for Dance & Theatre Studies at University College Bretton Hall. She trained at the Laban Art of Movement Centre and Goldsmiths College, University of London and received an MA in Performance Studies from New York University. At Bretton Hall she introduced the BA (Hons) Dance Degree in 1988 and the MA Contemporary Performing Arts (Dance) in 1994. She is a committee member of the European League of Institutes of the Arts (ELIA) Dance Section, a board member of Motionhouse Dance Theatre and Conference Director of *The Greenhouse Effect: the art and science of nurturing dance makers.*

Gill Clarke

Gill Clarke is an independent dance artist, a founder member of the Siobhan Davies Dance Company and previously dancer with Janet Smith. Her work as a freelance performer and choreographer includes ongoing projects with Rosemary Butcher and the Gandini Juggling Project. She teaches extensively in the UK and abroad for students, professionals and companies. In 1995 she directed the Choreographers and Composers Exchange and is frequent 'mentor' to emerging choreographers. She chairs the Thursday Group, a regular discussion forum for dance artists, and is closely involved with Chisenhale Dance Space - an artist-driven experimental space. She is a member of the executive of Dance UK and the British Association of Choreographers. Recently she co-authored, with Rachel Gibson, the "Independent Dance Review" for the Arts Council of England.

Matteo Fargion

Matteo Fargion was born in Milan, Italy in 1961 and is now based in London. He studied composition with Kevin Volans at the University of Natal, South Africa, and later with Howard Skempton in London. His music has been performed at music and dance venues throughout the world, and broadcast by several radio stations including BBC and Hessische Rundfunk. Since 1989, when he was selected to attend the Gulbenkian Course for Professional Composers and Choreographers, he has worked extensively in the dance field, collaborating with England's leading choreographers (eg Jonathan Burrows and Siobhan Davies) on at least 20 pieces. He has also written music for 5 prize winning films, all by British director Adam Roberts.

Recent premieres include his chamber opera *Le Bellezze d'Hortensia* at the Theaterhaus in Stuttgart (co-production Akademie Schloss Solitude and Vielfaches Echo Festival), incidental music for the Staatstheater Stuttgart production of *Hedda Gabler* (directed by Elmar Goerden) and a piece for the Freiburg ensemble Quartett Avance at Darmstadt in July 1988. Current projects include 2 dance commissions for the Autumn season in England, a piece for Canadian pianist Stephen Clarke and a children's opera for the Neue Vokalsolisten, Stuttgart.

Kate Flatt

Kate Flatt trained at the Royal Ballet School, and the London School of Contemporary Dance. She studied choreography with Nina Fonaroff and Leonide Massine, for whom she worked as assistant. In 1978 she travelled to study traditional dance in its social and ritual context in Eastern Europe. Early choreographic work was as a British Independent, and broadened in to the fields of national and international opera, theatre and film. Her work includes *Turandot* for the Royal Opera and musical staging for the RSC's *Les Miserables*. In 1994 she created *The Dancing Room*, with Sally Jacobs, filmed for BBC2. She is now a Senior Lecturer at Middlesex University, a member of the Arts Council Advisory panel for dance and chair of the British Association of Choreographers.

Sue MacLennan

Sue MacLennan, choreographer, dancer and teacher, has, over the last twenty years, created an extensive body of work known for its celebratory physicality, thoughtful detail and sweeping gesture. Her choreography has been performed throughout Britain, in Europe, Australia and America. Sue has done much work to further collaborative work, with prominent artists from music, visual arts, theatre and the digital arts. She was a founder member of Chisenhale Dance Space, Artistic Director of *Moves Afoot* and *The Hothouse* for the South Bank's Purcell Room and is currently teaching choreography and improvisation at London Contemporary Dance School.

Sanjoy Roy

Sanjoy Roy studied dance at the Laban Centre, and received an MA in cultural studies from Goldsmiths College, University of London. He is co-editor and designer of *Dance Now*, and designs and edits publications for Dance Books Ltd. He has contributed to *Dance Now*, *Dance Theatre Journal*, *Animated* and the *International Dictionary of Modern Dance*, and is author of "Dirt, Noise, Traffic: Contemporary Indian Dance in the Western City" in *Dance in the City* ed Helen Thomas (Macmillan, 1997)

Contents

Introduction

The British Association of Choreographers and the Centre for Dance and Theatre Studies at Bretton Hall are delighted to collaborate on this *Dance Makers Portfolio*. It is one of several projects about choreographic development under the umbrella title of *The Greenhouse Effect: the Art and Science of Nurturing Dancemakers*, organised in partnership by Bretton Hall College of the University of Leeds and Yorkshire Dance, and sponsored by the National Lottery through the Arts Council of England and ELIA Thematic Network.

While much is written by dance historians and critics about the dance as choreographic product, little is known or shared about the intricacies of making new work, the intellectual endeavour, skills, social interaction or practical application of the choreographer and dancers. In this book experienced dance practitioners articulate their processes, giving access to their philosophies and approaches to dancemaking.

From two different standpoints, representing both the choreographic profession and the educators of future dance makers, BAC and the Centre attempt to answer a need for more readily available written documentation by choreographers currently working in Britain.

For students studying such a rapidly evolving art form, it is important to be in touch with the work of the present as well as the past. To have access not only to live and recorded performance, but also to the thinking and intentions of the artists making that work can enhance their understandings: of those individual pieces, of a choreographer's oeuvre, and also of the variety of approaches to the choreographic process in general.

For the art form itself to evolve, contemporary work needs to be considered and debated seriously - by fellow choreographers, by critics, audience, academics, teachers, promoters and funders. The perspective of those individual artists who currently make work is central here, and is one which may not have been generally available in text form.

Many of us have been lucky enough to be present, for example, at a post-performance discussion, when a choreographer has been inspiringly lucid about a dance work. How we have wished to take a few of those wise words away with us! We hope that the present collection will furnish some of these insights in more lasting form.

In terms of style and areas of artistic concern, we have been deliberately eclectic in our selection of choreographers. This diversity is mirrored in the presentation of each. We have been guided by the individual choreographer's wishes as to the format of their contribution.

Finally we would like to thank all the choreographers and interviewers who approached the project with such enthusiasm, and who have shared their experiences and insights so generously over the last few months. Equally our thanks go to all those who have given extra help with editing and to Val Oakes, Jean Roebuck and Beverley Smith who between them have transcribed literally hours of interviews.

Jo Butterworth and Gill Clarke.
September 1998

Peter Badejo
writes about dancemaking

Peter Badejo writes about dancemaking
June 1998

My Aims in Making Dance:

Dance I believe is a very strong expression of the circumstances and situation of a people. It communicates spoken and unspoken intentions. From the beginning of my dance career, I have always tried to represent in my work aspects of human existence that need attention. Sometimes this may be a commentary on the changes of the art itself, the influences and impact it may have on the people or just drawing attention to any issue I feel people may have overlooked. Coming from a culture where the arts function beyond the decorative and commercial, I find it difficult to base my art purely on aesthetics and the pursuit of economic or commercial reasons. *The premise for my work is the purpose of the message to be in the piece. The function is very essential.* Creating with the above considerations, my work tends to be very dramatic, extracting from life experiences, though not necessarily narrative. In situations where art has lost its link to everyday life, commercialisation becomes the main purpose of creation.

The act of composing African dance outside of Africa has impacted on the way I create movement and structure my dances. For instance, I have to take into consideration the audience here and what their understanding might be of the symbolic gesture and metaphor that I might wish to use in the piece. Furthermore, I might originally conceive the piece as being circular, but then have to adapt it to the square shape of the proscenium theatres here. I also tailor my movement vocabulary to suit British dancers to avoid having the movement looking as if it is 'grafted on' to them, since most dancers who practice African dance in this country are contemporary-trained and approach African dance from that perspective. Though their training helps them to quickly assess and learn dance movements, it does not give them an in-depth understanding of the dances. Added to the consideration above, the challenge then is to find a way of creating a product that is still African and yet expresses itself in contemporary language.

From comments generated by audiences on past performances, African dance audiences seem to be divided on their expectations of the dance form. There are those who still want African dance performances to fulfil their expectation of exoticism (sweaty bodies in grass skirts and all) and there are those who call for new expressions in African dance. This makes it more difficult when creating and presenting African dance forms to audiences in the West, especially those with pre-conceived notion of what dance from another culture is and should be.

'Sisi Agbe Aye'

In 1995, Badejo Arts continued to contribute to the on-going clarification and exploration of new language for African dance by staging a new production; *Sisi Agbe Aye.* After exploring and experimenting with two earlier productions, in search of a contemporary language, I sought collaboration with a choreographer who was interested in a similar goal. The aim was to find an artist that would have, in his past, used other cultures' performance influences in his work and would be searching for new expression in African dance. As usual, there was a lack of adequate resources, thus the devising and rehearsal of this piece was for only four weeks. In such a situation, the collaborating artist has to have the required knowledge to fully contribute to the making of the production.

Badejo Arts found and contacted Koffi Kokko, the renowned Benin-born international artist, to work with the company in the exploration of the theme. Koffi has taught many classes in England and some of his solo works have been shown in venues across England. His work is generated by oral tradition and nourished by ancient African art and philosophy. His credentials include choreography for companies internationally and his solo performances in Paris, Vienna, Spain and England. He has also studied with the renowned Alvin Ailey Dance Company in New York and has worked with French, German and Japanese choreographers. With the above experience, he has been able to use dance language in his work that is contemporary, and yet African in expression.

After I briefed Koffi on the theme and concept of the piece, he expressed his concern on the short period for the devising and rehearsal of the piece and the amount of information and new materials we required the dancers to take on in such a short period. The collaboration started with discussions on the theme, theoretically analysing the concept and looking at the possible ways of achieving the practicality of the concept in four weeks without compromising our aims and objectives. These early discussion meetings gave clarity to our approach to the creation of the work.

The piece *Sisi Agbe Aye* was based on the exploration of the inner contents of the (Agbe) gourd or calabash. Agbe Aye is a metaphor for the womb of the world. The gourd contains a multitude of seeds which grow into diverse forms, in the same way as human beings develop different characteristics and personalities. The theme was to shed light on or re-emphasise the differences in human characters and personalities. As characters and personalities differ, so do the movement expressions vary in African people's dance, and this makes generalisation incorrect. This concept was explained to the dancers in detail, and when the creation process began the dancers had a path to follow regarding the piece.

Each day of rehearsal started with a class, each of the choreographers teaching their style of movements. After the class, the creative work on the piece began. Each choreographer was responsible for different sections of the piece with the other observing and contributing where necessary, and rehearsals were taken alternatively between the choreographers using the same dancers.

Koffi and I have similar working methods in that we both use traditional African dance vocabulary as our point of departure. Also, we both work in similar ways with dancers, starting with what they know and are capable of doing, and then moving them on to what is totally new to them. We either taught pre-choreographed pieces or gave the dancers improvisational exercises using the various concepts in the theme as stimuli. At the end of each day different sections of the work were brought together and discussed in a group and changes made if necessary. Towards the end of the four weeks the various segments were brought together and rehearsed for flow.

There were times slated for the dancers to work with both choreographers simultaneously on experiments. These times were mainly for dancers to explore with the choreographers how to create movements based on the knowledge of other cultures. Three sections of the production were worked on in this way: the scene that explored the way in which other dance forms such as Jazz came out of African dance, then the scene in which each dancer externalised his or her personal religious experience, and the various experiments with music or sounds to create moods.

For the dancers, the challenge was learning two styles of African dance from two choreographers simultaneously. Though Koffi and I generate our movements from the Yoruba tradition, we come from different parts of West Africa and therefore have different influences in our movement. Furthermore, our approaches to choreography are different, based on the influences of where we had studied and those we had worked with as dancers or choreographers. Koffi tends to be linear in his work, whilst I am more circular in my use of formation and movement.

In the beginning of the piece, the collaboration was a bit difficult since in previous productions the decisions were made unilaterally, whereas, with the collaboration, consideration was given to others' opinions and conclusions were thus not easy to arrive at. However, the work became richer as we progressed due to the incorporation of the other artist's ideas. For example, the use of certain movements was a daily discussion until it was agreed that we should not define movements in isolation but look at them in the context of the piece.

At a point in our experimenting and improvising we needed to define what differentiates a contemporary African movement from a non-African contemporary movement. We both arrived at the conclusions that the 'identity' of an African movement resided in its execution being inseparable from rhythm. One can perceive the rhythm that should accompany an African movement whether it is performed to music or not. This intimacy is not present in western movement forms.

In the production, gourds were constructed as props and sets to symbolically represent the seeds of the gourd; these were mobile, so that they could be moved around the stage by the dancers to represent changes in place and mood. The lighting design worked very well with this creating a sense of unpredictability and uncertainty of what could emerge from the seedlings when out of the pods.

The costumes were designed to enhance the meaning of the production. As much as we got the costume designer to relate to an 'African' colour concept, we made sure that the effect did not distort the production. Several African productions are described as colourful with very little meaning for the usage. In *Sisi Agbe* attention was paid to the colour and materials used to reflect the intention of the piece. Also, extreme care was taken in the design and utilisation of costumes.

In my own consideration one of the most successful sections of the piece was a duet put together by Koffi and I. Using traditional movement experiences as a basis for improvisation, each of us explored the journey of two strangers in a strange and hostile environment. Rhythm created while performing this section contrasted sharply with the melodic sounds of the mbira (a lute musical instruction) recital. This contrast added to the harshness created.

The result of the collaboration was a complete departure from my earlier productions and the reactions from the audiences were of mixed feelings. Some appreciated the fresh ideas in the work and the attempt in searching for new expressions. Some comment was that the production needed more dancing with energy than the dramatic movements. The music was said to be very powerful and creative. Again, this indicated the readiness of the audience to accept innovations in music more than in dance.

The collaboration was a learning process for all that were involved. I hope to further explore and incorporate in future choreography some of the ideas tried out in this work. I discovered how time consuming it is to work in this way, that is in a collaborative mode. The time consuming nature of this particular style of production was also emphasised by the limit of just four weeks that we had to conceive and rehearse the piece. I felt that aspects of the piece could have been developed more if time permitted. The dancers were still grappling with the movement even at the last day of rehearsal, making it difficult for them to internalise and become comfortable with the movements. The result of this work makes it even more apparent that a proper training resource is needed for the development of African dance techniques if innovative works are expected from the work. There is the need to have the resources to create the space and time to experiment, gamble and grapple with new forms in African dance techniques. More so because as mentioned earlier there is no such beauty or beast as a homogeneous African dance form, for as illustrated, even within one specific ethnic culture there are various types and modes of dance all with different specific ** ritualistic purposes or messages. They are different modes of communication.

Ritual here denotes the celebratory aspect of my culture and many African cultures, and not necessarily related to Juju or Voodoo as popularly conceived in the West.

David Bintley
in conversation with Kate Flatt

David Bintley in conversation with Kate Flatt
May 1998

Kate: *How do you get going on a work? Where do you start?*

David: You know, that's the worst question you can ask!

Kate: *Maybe, but perhaps we could focus on a particular work? Where do the ideas come from and how do you begin to put them into practice?*

David: Firstly people and priorities change, and I am a very different person now to maybe fifteen years ago. Then, I was primarily driven by just movement, its shapes and musical forms. For me those early thematic works were as abstract as I got if you like. But now I am much more driven by ideas. In Tavener's *Protecting Veil* for example there is a very strong idea which is pictorial and spiritual, yet it is not a narrative. This is very different from *Edward II* which is inspired by seeing the play, and not liking either the play or the production. It was one of those occasions when you realize that it would be perfect for dance. It was the same with *Hobson's Choice*, suddenly I could see how to make it; I was trying to make a Mozart opera, a Mozart comedy in dance.

Kate: *Tell me more about Protecting Veil.*

David: Tavener has based the work around the life of the Virgin Mary, and it's is in the form of icons, just snap shots. You can listen to it as pure music and yet it is terribly emotional, because of its subject matter. What I really relish about *Protecting Veil* is that it is both dramatic and very abstract and that Tavener deals with it in a way as a ritual.

Kate: *So are the ritual elements how you could connect up with the work?*

David: I think ritual is obviously very important and always has been in the history of dance. It has also affected me in different ways.

Kate: *How did you go about transmitting your reactions to the piece, the icons, and sense of ritual into movement?*

David: I wanted to do it and yet couldn't work out how. I wanted to present it with extraordinary simplicity, but I didn't want it to be a school nativity play. I didn't want to do it with characters, so I had the idea of the veil itself. In terms of the ritual this is a real thing that is passed from on woman to another, to diffuse the narrative, if you like. Each woman becomes the Virgin Mary. There are different celebrations, events that women go through at different stages of their life. It's funny how many images came out of working with the dancers, and the simple idea that the veil could become anything.

Kate: *So with the veil idea, the catalyst to the invention, how did the ideas and images unfold?*

David: I was in danger of getting lumbered with a prop which is integral to the work and yet could dominate. I used it in a variety of ways. It became the journey on the donkey, instead of Mary literally being on the donkey. I used it bunched up at one point, held against her stomach which was her pregnancy. I used it as a covering for the window that the Angel Gabriel appeared at. She was standing by the window and he just drops in. It became the veil that shrouds her at the cross; the cloth which Christ was buried in and which was lifted off him for the resurrection. Then it was very simply placed around her neck for the domination. She holds it in a way that makes her appear old. The dancer is a very young, very beautiful girl, and yet she looks like she is eighty. There is one literally inspired moment where just before she dies, an angelic Christ figure appears with all of the apostles who have returned for Mary's death, and she is reaching out to him, with the 'veil' wrapped around her so that she is almost horizontal leaning toward him. The veil becomes the gulf between life and death. I love it when I get inspiration.

Kate: *Do you feel you have to plan a lot before you go into rehearsal?*

David: I don't plan so much any more, except you do need a point at which to start. You can't come in and spend ten minutes thinking about what to begin with and obviously if you are dealing with lots of people it's best to have some ideas just to keep the room in order. It doesn't worry me if I spend a day and don't get any inspirations, I know there is more time tomorrow. Sometimes it is as quick to find out what you don't want to do as it is to know what you do want.

Kate: *Which brings us on to working conditions. As the Director of a company, are you able to create the conditions you need?*

David: Yes, it's wonderful, it's why I am doing it. I realised that unless I had a director who was completely sympathetic and in tune with what I was doing, I would constantly come up against problems. The great thing is not "Here I am, I can do what the hell I like", because you can't. It would be really wrong of me to dominate the repertoire, but I do get to choose which works go together. I have been quite frustrated in the past when I have made something specifically to finish a programme, and it ends up being placed at the beginning.

Kate: *How about choosing dancers?*

David: It is different when you are running the show, because you can pick who you like, but give everyone a chance and work with everyone.

Kate: *How did you come to choose the lead girl for Protecting Veil?*

David: Well originally I had cast from the principals, with two very bright girls as covers, to give them a go. When it came to it, two of them were injured and so the starring role went to Isabel McMeekan, a nineteen year old from the corps de ballet, who I would not normally have scheduled. What I was asking of her was enormous. Most of the work had been set on others, but very roughly, and it was that period two weeks before the premiere when you really start getting it down and running it. She has a seven minute solo, with the solo cello, which is extraordinarily difficult. The girl I had made it on is wonderful, in her late twenties and more experienced, so it was very difficult for this younger girl who was very nervous. But it was fine and I think it was a character-forming experience for her.

Kate: *Can you think of a particular working relationship with a dancer that has taken you somewhere?*

David: I absolutely make the dance for who is in front of me, but I have to think ahead in a company such as Birmingham Royal Ballet. You are not just planning the best for a particular evening, but having to think not only of the second night, but three casts ahead, even several years ahead. It can be difficult for a second cast, because you are perhaps asking them to follow someone who has an idiosyncratic way of moving. Leticia Muller for instance has a miraculous ports de bras and use of the upper back so I scarcely choreograph for that area because she does it for me. That can be very difficult for another dancer to follow sometimes.

Kate: *Is there a guiding mechanism in you, of where you want to go with the dance material?*

David: I do know what I want, and I only have recourse to ask somebody else if I am not sure. But late on in making a piece the doubts can start to creep in.

Kate: *The doubt thing. What causes that?*

David: The hardest thing is keeping a perspective on the piece, by not getting too close so that you can't see what is going on. Then you can get filled with doubt which can be quite profitable but also painful. Because you do your hour and a half rehearsal and then you've got the other twenty two and a half to cope with. With no feedback it is very difficult. I do rely very much on a notator, the ballet master or mistress or whoever is in rehearsal. I might turn to them and ask what they think, if I am genuinely not sure. Sometimes you don't like something and want to scrap the whole thing and they say no no no... At others you look round and maybe they are sitting there behind you looking a bit bored that day...

Kate: *Do you find it hard to bridge the distance between the vulnerability of the studio and the demands of directing the company?*

David: I think it is part and parcel of the dual role that I fulfil here in that the director is the last person to find out anything. I can make a whole piece like **Protecting Veil** and get no response from the dancers at all. In fact **Protecting Veil** was made over a long period, so that sponsors could come in and watch. I started in November and did half a solo and then got to about three weeks before the premiere in May and spoke with Dennis Bonner (notator) "You know I've done half an hour of this piece and yet I don't feel like I've started." It was because I hadn't had that initial couple of weeks trying to find the vocabulary. Once you have it you can steam towards the end. It was fine eventually, but difficult.

Kate: *When devising your narrative works like Edward II and Hobson's Choice did you have any dramaturgical help?*

David: No, I do it myself.

Kate: *What do you find is the hardest thing about it?*

David: I think it is easier if you are starting from scratch with an idea, you can do what you want, but it is hard to get a scenario right. You constantly come up against blocks. I am planning a new work now and have been working away at it for years and years. I suddenly had a moment of inspiration here in my office when everything fell into place in about half an hour. It isn't just perseverance. You have to get something from somewhere sometimes... With a work like Edward II you spend so long in preparation and know the music so well that actually choreographing the work is somehow not difficult. You have almost visualised the piece into existence. It is much harder to work with existing music like Tavener's.

Kate: *Is all of your preparation, the complete breakdown of the story, on paper?*

David: Yes. It's a very tight structure before I get together with the composer. It will be an accurate moment to moment breakdown with timings and everything. Then it is theirs. When it comes back, it all changes again. John McCabe has this way which is quite exciting, because you get an immediate overview. He takes a number and just has a germ of an idea and then each section grows by itself. It might be a simple rhythmic idea, or a melodic idea, as little as a bar or two of different ideas that he likes, which will grow into the one we use. They naturally go into each other or there might be a bridging passage. I have an overview so that I can see what the whole thing might become. We have a musical idea for virtually every moment of the work even if it is only a few bars.

Kate: *Do you have any input into the orchestration, or a feeling about the instrumental colour?*

David: No, that is up to the composer as it is their choice and I wouldn't presume. The only thing that I don't like is a slow pas de deux on the oboe! I'm not an oboe fan. Clarinet perhaps. If I go to any composer it's with the knowledge of what they do. I don't say to John, "I love all this modern stuff you do but I really want some Tchaikovsky". Once I've given him my ideas, he writes and then it will tend to change my ideas. I recently went to spend a few hours with him and he played me something that was nothing like what I expected. But with a bit of thought I realised it was better. That I wouldn't need to portray a particular moment because the music does it for me.

Kate: *What about the music dance relationship? How does that evolve?*

David: If John plays me a musical idea and it's got a recognisable rhythm or impulse that I feel sure that I can dance to, then what I will really listen for is the way that he is conveying the narrative. Initially you have to keep a sort of pulse check on whether you can dance to it, if it is a good shape, or is it a little too obvious.

Kate: *Would the timings fluctuate once you are in the working process?*

David: In a small way. Like shifting the comparative importance of a particular number by putting four minutes for a pas de deux rather than one and a half for a duet. I have to keep a balance, some kind of overall check on the time and to know whether it's two or three acts. You have to have an eye on the clock. With Paul Reade, composer for *Hobson's Choice*, we prepared every number. He would not commit to paper until we had virtually verified every detail. I hardly needed a recording because I knew each piece as I went along.

Kate: *Do you work chronologically?*

David: No, I don't need to work chronologically, but I need to go from a point which I know is going to continue to lead me on. With *Edward II* there is a fifteen minute scene which is a duet for two women which goes on to a pas de deux for a man and a woman. This then becomes a pas de trois man, woman, man, which turns into a pas de deux for two men. It was clearly the point to start with because there are only three people to work with and I could get some kind of vocabulary going and a quarter of an hour of the piece done.

Kate: *Is the storytelling the driving force?*

David: All the time I am thinking, does this work for the narrative? It sounds as if the narrative is more important than the dance, but it isn't. It is just that I have to know that, in the simplest of terms, it is danceable. I think that is something that only choreographers who work in narrative dance can understand. People who don't have a great understanding about dance say that it is just stories. Its like saying that Mozart wrote *Marriage of Figaro* just because he thought it was a good story. No, it's an opera. Some people say that *Hobson's Choice* is a musical or *Edward II* is great "theatre". It's not true. What I do can only be done by dancers through dance. In *Hobson's Choice* every second is a ballet. In the work there is a plot outline and then the movement outline, where the meaning is somehow more evident than it is in spoken text. With *Edward II* the characters are brought to life through poetry and although it sounds arrogant, I think you can go beyond the words and add to what is there. I'm not ransacking English literature, I choose these things because they can work well in dance.

Kate: *In Hobson's Choice you used ballet vocabulary, which is not everyday movement, in a very natural and unobtrusive way.*

David: Yes I try to make it seamless. Everything in nineteenth century ballet was completely broken up, like old style opera. There were rituals in the form of processions, arrivals, and the setting up of moments. I don't think we can go back to showing those formal structures as they did in the nineteenth century. There has to be structure but it has to be hidden all the time. I still think of that very strongly even in a through narrative. By that I mean a dance where I never consider including something that is extraneous, or there for decoration. Even a divertissement has to have a narrative purpose or be saying something, like the park scene in **Hobson's Choice**. Some critics called it padding, as if one would ever want to pad anything. What is important is that it gets us out of the shop, and that it is about the social milieu. The two sisters are annoyed because Will was with Maggie in the park, as mentioned in the play, and you have to see what cannot be put into words. Their encounter appears out of place, because everyone meeting and dancing in the park is better dressed than Will is. It emphasises the difference in social status.

Kate: *Tell me about your background research and reading.*

David: Reading is very important, especially history. I read about the whole period for a piece, for example the Dark Ages for **Edward II**. I am interested in traditional customs and things that have been lost. I used that for **Far From the Madding Crowd**. I love English dance, particularly Morris Dance, it is fantastic stuff. I've used it in **Still Life at the Penguin Café** and **Hobson's Choice** but it comes into everything. If I hadn't been a choreographer I could have been a popular historian.

Kate: *What about future plans?*

David: I am planning two full length works based on Arthurian legends. This has been a lifelong passion inherited from my mother. There was a big flurry of interest when a new edition of Mallory came out. I started work in 1980 and realised that I couldn't even scrape the surface with a full length ballet. It would take two or three at least. Fine, I thought, and suddenly being in charge of a place like this it becomes possible. It is a luxury but it all works with the Millenium and for many reasons. It is scheduled for 2000 and it will close and re-open Birmingham for the new building re-development. I think given the situation we have to make a bit of a splash, so Arthur is the splash.

Christopher Bruce
in conversation with Gill Clarke

Christopher Bruce in conversation with Gill Clarke June 1998

The making of Swansong.

Gill: *I am interested about your motivation for Swansong. You had already demonstrated very clearly that a piece could have a powerful political message through Ghost Dances and I wondered whether there was a coming together of events and influences at this particular time that made you want to make this piece.*

Christopher: Well, I had the idea for a long time. When I make a piece that, as you say, has a strong social or political message, and having chosen the subject that might be my basic discipline for the piece, what I'm interested in is making a dance, making a piece of theatre which will engage an audience and make them feel something. So the subject matter and material that I make is there for that end.

I think *Swansong* started with a combination of things. Mentally I was already quite involved with the plight of political prisoners, and then I read a book called *A Man* by Oriana Falacci which greatly affected me. It talked in great and graphic detail about the actual interrogation and torture, and just the loneliness and where the mind goes to when a person is in solitary confinement for long periods of time. I previously had the idea that I would like to choreograph it almost as a piece of Commedia dell'Arte, that is to have a collection of clowns telling the story, because what I liked about the Commedia was that in its heyday it was actually politically and socially a very important commentary on the times, particularly on what was happening at court. And I loved that idea. After the 18th century it tended to dissipate towards the 'end of the pier' pantomime and became just a pretty amusement, whereas I think that when Glen Tetley made *Pierrot Lunaire* he was adhering much more to the fundamentals of Commedia dell'Arte and commenting very seriously on life, and the characters there were metaphors in a sense.

So, I had the idea to do a piece almost like a slapstick number, which actually was a black comedy. I think I was very much affected by the work I'd done in the theatre and was attracted by methods of working with actors. My pieces are very often a form of directed drama where the movement is the script. That was basically my starting point, and very simply I took three clowns, a Pierrot figure, the Arlecchino and the bullying Brighella. I did toy for a long time with the idea of keeping them in clown costumes, and I would still like to see a performance like that. Of course, it still involves the red nose and the clowning, and I thought it would give it a different connotation if I dressed them as, for example, South American policemen and then just the prisoner would be dressed very simply in jeans. It could be just any kid picked up off the street, because what occurred to me was that often the people that were picked up and tortured had done nothing, they couldn't tell any secrets because they didn't have any to tell.

So, that was basically the beginning. Whenever I do a piece, I'm very severe in the limitations I put on the material, and in the way that the vocabulary relates to the particular piece. There are certainly themes in many of my pieces and movements that re-occur, but I shape them more or less to create a language for that particular piece. Later I may touch on that subject again and develop it slightly, either distil it or abstract it more, or make it fuller in its narrative quality.

Gill: *Does that sense come before you get into the studio, or is that one of the tasks you give yourself while you are working?*

Christopher: Well before I went into the studio I thought about the structure and movement. Though, much as I might have planned certain sequences of movement, - as soon as I start working in the studio that preplanned movement changes because I often throw away the first "word" I thought of as it were, and the journey with the dancers takes me into another direction. Therefore, suddenly I feel naked again, in that I have nothing to lean back on except what I create in that time and space. This is very hard – I make myself very vulnerable. I allow myself to be influenced by what happens in the moment, and sometimes it can be very destructive if it doesn't work. At other times it can take me on a journey I could not have pre-conceived. But I still stick to my ground rules, so it limits my choice. I remember Bob Cohan saying that choreography is a question of choices; you've got a whole repertoire of movements you can choose from, anything. But you have got to make the correct choice, and I think what is wrong with work that I have seen over the years is that I see streams and streams of quite inventive, well composed movement but I feel no real purpose for it to be there. Often not only does it have no purpose but also there is no development or theme adhered to, and it is as if choreographers have just gone anywhere with the movement. They haven't been disciplined enough.

Gill: *Can you describe a little bit more, when you first began this piece, what the limitations might have been?*

Christopher: Well let's take the vaudeville material for the interrogation. Can we suggest questions and answers in tap through the sounds we make on the floor? What was wonderful was that we discovered that we really could make tap sound like words. So those rhythms and sounds were the basis for a vaudeville language including tap and a form of jazz: what I call "language of the banal", in the same way that Kurt Weill and Brecht used the banal to say very serious things in those early satirical music theatre pieces. So their language was one that the audience would relate to and remember. It has comedy and it has humour because the more you make people laugh, the easier it is to make them cry. It is a basic theatrical device one incorporates.

When the prisoner is answering the interrogators he's talking the same language. When he is left alone in the cell, the movement is much more about imagery and the imagery is about escape. For example, there's the focal point of the light or a window which is freedom, so the movement has a sailing, flying quality like a bird in flight interrupted by trapped animal images. But I wanted to have something that was quite pure; therefore it is full of quite abstract and classical lines, the arabesque. I also wanted to make it very demanding, very challenging technically, so I gave the character all these difficult balances where he had to fight for balance and this creates tension in itself – trying to get on top of something. So for the prisoner alone it was a combination of very classical lines with more contemporary but very lyrical movements contrasted with tortured arm movements. Then the final solo where he leaves the chair, the tap dancing is just like a fleeting thought during a slow progression toward the light and finally escaping.

Swansong was made at a time in my life when I was really saying goodbye to performing. I was still going through the difficult process of having to leave it behind, knowing that when it was gone it was gone forever. And because the piece is, obviously, a dance piece, with a dance language, the metaphor that I was working on was about being able to free myself from the torture and the discipline of dance and being able to walk through that window and leave it all behind me. So I related the two – the very personal experience of freeing myself from something which gave me pleasure and pain, with the analogy of the prisoner in the cell, and that basically is the material and the nuts and bolts of the structure.

Gill:	So in the making process, how does the piece gradually evolve? Do you start from the beginning and work your way through?
Christopher:	Yes I do. I tend to because my journey often deviates from a pre-conceived plan, and I may have a better idea along the road. So I do sometimes work on different sections like in *Sergeant Early's Dream* where I knew basically what I wanted to do with the dancers and where the characters and situations were already formed by the songs chosen. I could work out a sequence and allocate two hours with this duet and an hour on that solo because I can only work for so long on one section before I get bogged down. The change refreshes...
Gill:	And what about the actual making process? Do you now make less of the movement yourself or do you do that just as much as ever?
Christopher:	I make movement but I cannot demonstrate as fully as I used to and I find that very frustrating. I'm trying to make it a positive thing. I use my dancers more and I find myself using movement shorthand or marking, more often.
Gill:	Do you develop a very clear physical sensation or an image of the movement you want?
Christopher:	Absolutely, I mean, I make the movement, I just can't always dance everything. I still do a great deal but I simply can't do it all and that's been a source of frustration. The question over the last few years — because of the battle with the effects of polio — is whether I could actually go on making work, because when you've got one leg which is nerve damaged you cannot do as much as before, and you get more and more out of shape. But in a sense I think that having to fight against that all of my creative life has actually helped me to do the things I've done. It's always been hard for me, and I've always had to find ways of dealing with a disability which has grown more serious as I've grown older. So right from the beginning it was there and gave me a kind of drive, whereas I've seen people so talented physically with such easy techniques that they almost seemed to get bored. Whereas I notice that the people who don't have ideal bodies or strong techniques really have to fight for what they do, and they become more mature and much more interesting artists. Think of Marie Rambert (Mim) who never had the first choice of bodies, as De Valois had, so Mim had to make dancers out of less than perfect techniques and she made the most wonderful dancers. When I joined the company in 1963, there were

qualities and a depth not often found in the bigger classical companies, like some of the mature people in this company today, and like yourself and others in Sue's (Siobhan Davies') company.

Gill: *To return to Swansong, often you start with a piece of music but this time it was a commissioned score.*

Christopher: Yes I started with no music, and Philip Chambon just came and watched with his stopwatch and sometimes his tape recorder, and what was wonderful about my collaboration with Philip was that we kept leapfrogging each other, each being inspired by the other. Collaborations don't always work out perfectly but I would say that in this case it was really satisfying. For example, in the second movement I just sang *Tea for Two* and he constructed a tune with the same rhythm; and then for the cane dance section I suggested something with a South American sound, and then he developed that into the panpipe notes of the last solo. It is quite a long piece but I wanted to make them feel that this prisoner was really going through a long process. I went back to one of my sources, Panagoulis, whose experiences are documented in *A Man* – the years in prison, being abused and months and months alone in solitary confinement – to get the feeling of that terrible frustration of dealing with time and loneliness. Therefore the piece had to be taken to the limit in terms of duration. I wanted to convey the idea that the actions were occurring over a long period of time. That is why I slow the pace down for the solo in silence, but for the noise of the chair being dragged or banged on the floor. It pushes the audiences' patience maybe, but it works because of the change of pace for the cane dance. Rather like the way, halfway through *Cruel Garden* between the cafe scene and Buster Keaton, we slowed the pace. It is dangerous because it is at a point where the audience have been sitting for some time, and if they are going to lose concentration, that is where it will happen. However, if they can stay with it, the coming changes in dynamic will carry them through to the end. Control of pace is a basic theatrical device that you need to manage in any long or major piece.

Gill: *And with an element of humour as well?*

Christopher: Yes, the more you make them laugh the more you make them feel uncomfortable later when the situation turns nasty, and you know, I don't always plan those moments – they come to me very intuitively during the process of creation. I trust my instinct, although occasionally it will let me down, but I just think that when I do get it right it enables me to create something that has

29

a special quality, and do something every four or five pieces that really touches people.

Gill: *So did that really clear sense of dramatic pacing come first time?*

Christopher: Yes, I think it did. I cut the last solo and made it shorter. I didn't quite get the shape of that right.

Gill: *And in terms of the music, it seems to me that the sense of limitation or spareness you were talking about with the movement is the real strength of the sound too. Did Philip need to pare away the music?*

Christopher: Yes, Philip is incredibly instinctive, you know. You hardly have to say anything to him.

Gill: *How has the piece changed with different dancers, different companies over the years?*

Christopher: Each cast is different. The problem has always been to have a dancer performing the prisoner/victim figure that can cope technically and dramatically with the demands of the piece. The thing about Koen Onzo, the original boy, was that he had such an all-round ability. He was a very beautiful, classical premier dancer who had an ability to move. There were times when I used to get irritated because he made it look a bit more like ballet than I intended, but it didn't matter, he made the meaning clear. There have been other people who have understood more of the contemporary quality but not had the classical line. And that is why I then enjoyed very much working on the piece with women, because they do have that classical line to start with. The problem is that it needs such strength and stamina that it is a very cruel, demanding piece for anyone to dance, particularly for a woman. I have looked at ways of trying to make it easier for the women, as I see no reason why women shouldn't perform it.

Gill: *Does it read as a very different piece?*

Christopher: I think it reads as the same piece, but it is like an entirely different cast doing a play, they just bring their own interpretation to it. With women it tends not to be so physical and brutal, but slightly more gentle, more lyrical in feeling. It can also be more sinister and cruel and it seems that men feel particularly uneasy when they watch the women do it. What I don't do is to cast two men and a woman, because the sexual connotation would be all wrong, though it works with one male and one female interrogator and with a female victim. Technically, having a man in there helps with the speed of some of the lifts. In reality men do interrogate women and, of course, it is part of systematic torture that women do get raped, but I didn't want to suggest that idea very obviously, I wanted it to be a little bit more ambiguous. I prefer it to be three men or three women ideally. But in all the places it's been done, Houston, Berlin, here, Geneva, each cast has had its own nuances.

Gill: *You revive pieces frequently. Do you want to interfere and change things?*

Christopher: I do want to interfere. It is like putting on the same suit of clothing for another person. I feel the need to cut the suit accordingly, therefore, it remains essentially the same piece but I will change little bits. I often do anyway when I revive things, not too much, but there are always moments that I don't think I ever got right, so I have another attempt. And, there are certain things that you need to change for a particular artist.

Gill: *Do you ever look back at a piece and think "well that's what I would have done then, but now I would do something different," or do you feel that pieces in a way are timeless, that its just individual personalities of the dancers that change it?*

Christopher: I think the pieces that I do remain alive, they must have a timeless quality in a sense. Like in performing *Cruel Garden* again, the ingredients still work. We can see that it is a piece from the 70s, but I have ignored opportunities to update things choreographically. With this particular piece I have changed things as time has gone by but maintained the style, not only of how I was choreographing then, but how I was choreographing for Lindsay's style of work. If it got too sophisticated it just looked wrong. It wasn't right for a Kemp production.

Gill: *Is there ever anything in the transition of a piece from studio to stage that takes you by surprise?*

Christopher: Every time. Its always a shock and generally I think "this isn't working" because I've got so used to seeing it in the studio. On the other hand, I do get some pleasant surprises and think "oh that looks better," but the initial reaction is usually a negative one.

Gill: *And has it frequently changed from the idea you had at the beginning? You implied that in a sense you do let yourself be led in a different direction in the studio.*

Christopher: Structurally I know what I am doing before I go into the studio, and also the language I am going to use, but the piece is created together with the dancers. I think I'm led by my instincts and by what I discover in the studio, but the theme and main drive usually remain the same.

Gill: *How much do you find it useful to let the dancers in on those themes and undercurrents to the work?*

Christopher: I usually let them know, though not always right at the beginning. I give the dancers an idea about what its about and what I'm doing, but I don't give them too much detail until I get really started on the piece and then, when I know where I'm going, if I know where I'm going, I explain more.

Gill: *And is that because somehow you think they would almost start trying to lead you there too soon, or by a different route?*

Christopher: Yes, I want the freedom to change things. I don't want to give them too many pre-conceived ideas because they might just get into the cliches you're trying to avoid. It is difficult to avoid them because we've gone through such a rich period of dance and we've seen so much over the last 50 years. So, I'm just trying to find something new, to trust my instinct, that is hard.

Gill: *Returning to a theme, does that reflect something to you about how your concerns have changed over a period of time?*

Christopher: Its funny how my concerns tend to be the same. I think they are more thought through now, but I think in many ways I'm the same person I was in my mid-twenties. You know I was very absorbed by the innocence of children and by watching children play in relation to growing up. Now I know more about growing up and people in general, and I think through very simple means you can really tell universal stories. I love making movements. I think in some ways it would have been easier writing poems if that had been my vocabulary, but writing plays with movement has always been something that has caught me and I love its possibility for ambiguity.

Gill: *Are you suggesting that the word might have been an easier medium to do what you want to do?*

Christopher: Maybe, but I enjoy the challenge of trying to say it in movement.

Gill: *Because your themes, ideas and stories are universal, the pieces are in a sense more dramatic than abstract, would you say?*

Christopher:	Yes, I'm interested in people. I choose movement because I like making dances; but it also seems that I feel the need to say something about humanity, about what I feel, and those concerns haven't changed all that much in 30 years.

Gill: *You mentioned before we began the tensions of trying to retain a creative focus at the same time as running a company. How, between making pieces, do you try and safeguard that? What inspires you or stimulates or feeds you between pieces? What might spark off the seed of the next piece?*

Christopher: Well you know, although its a hard, grinding, challenging job and there are a lot of difficulties one has to deal with, I find running a company ultimately very creative, whether its making a programme, bringing choreographers in or getting the enjoyment of seeing the company and the organisation perform. I never know quite where the next seed is coming from. I mean there are always a few seeds floating around, a few pieces of music that have excited me, a few vague theatrical ideas, dramatic ideas that need to be developed.

Gill: *Do you go and see theatre? Do you read a lot?*

Christopher: I read a great deal. I go to the theatre. I don't go to a great many concerts but I listen to music all the time. Many of my ideas come from literature. I read voraciously but I see films less and less as I feel there is so little worth seeing. Of course, I do see quite a lot of dance but I find it not good to see too much. How do critics do it, I mean how can they not be jaded?

Gill: *What about the constant creative dilemma to renew yourself, and working with the same group of dancers to renew them, or to get them to help renew you?*

Christopher: Well, I've worked with so many different people. I still keep my association with Houston. I've worked with so many companies over the last few years, that actually I find it quite enjoyable to be just working with this group at Rambert. And it is changing; it is a big company so I work with a range of people and develop a relationship with all the dancers. I have the choice of doing either one or two pieces a year. Last year I didn't do a new work at all. Now I would like to spend more time being creative, whether it's here or elsewhere. I feel that I've got the company on to a certain footing, have a wonderful team working for me and am delegating more and more responsibility so that I am freer for the next few years to create more. Actually, if I haven't created anything for a year and half then I feel quite rusty choreographically – I find it's a tortuous process. I try to enjoy it and there are moments of incredible pleasure when something works, but it is a struggle.

Gill: *Are these moments of struggle usually the things that create the breakthroughs to different planes?*

Christopher: Yes, nothing comes easily. Beware when it is all flowing; you look back on it and think "it's all a load of rubbish - let's start again." We need the courage to throw things out and start again, even when we know we've got a time limit.

One thing I'm really interested in is seeing whether I can tell a story in movement engaging other aspects of theatre, using the spoken word, the dancer singing, in a sense as in **Cruel Garden** but in an entirely different language. I think I've been affected by the work I've done in musical theatre, and probably from the frustration of only being the choreographer and not actually being in charge of the whole direction. It's not that I want to create a musical, but I'd like to make a piece that incorporates some of those disciplines.

Although I see myself very much as an artist born of traditional disciplines, and however much I've been influenced by the contemporary dance languages that I've experienced, from Graham to Limon to Cunningham, the root of my work lies in the original classical ballet technique and the disciplines of the theatre. Those are the foundations of Rambert Dance Company. So I work out of that tradition as it were, even if I take it and extend it in a different direction. I see myself as a contemporary choreographer based in those traditional disciplines. I'm influenced by many other things, of course, forms of theatre as well as dance, but that is my root. I would love to try to find a new language to tell a story. I've done it in little detailed sections within my pieces, but at present I am interested in developing this idea. Also I love to create dances that give pleasure, I love theatre that engages and I enjoy being able to involve and touch an audience. The challenge of attempting to do this successfully is probably what drives me.

Gill: *The proliferation of dance languages at the moment, do you see that almost as a weakness, that there somehow isn't enough of a solid root or tradition?*

Christopher: I find there's a kind of looseness in compositional terms; the language can be quite inventive but often lacks purpose. I sometimes question why the work exists at all.

Gill:	*Is that more to do with structure do you think, than language?*

Christopher:	I think too many choreographers are embarking on a choreographic career too soon; they should be gaining as much experience in the profession as possible and watching and learning from others, getting to know what it feels like to dance the work of others, and then when they have some maturity and they have some backup, some foundation, start creating their own vocabulary. There's no harm in learning the art of composition early on. I wish I had had the classes that people come out of certain schools with now, armed with that ability. I had to learn about structure and vocabulary just by observing and experimenting. One taught oneself and observed other people's work. Now students get lessons and the chance to practice at school. That's wonderful. But I think its almost as though they don't have enough of a foundation, their work has no root and, therefore, however, inventive or talented some people are, you find that they do one or two pieces and then one never hears of them again. They have no chance to build up a repertoire of work because they use all their abilities in the first two pieces. I just feel you have to have lived a little bit, and had some experience. It's not enough to be quite inventive and just be very physical – and then they are often crushed by rejection. I think this is why, when I look at what is being made and who is really making interesting work which has depth, it is still the middle and older generations that interest me.

Gill:	*Do you think that it is also the fault of the systems, whether it be promoters or funders, picking people up too soon, looking for something new and different...*

Christopher:	I think we're all so desperate to find the next generation of choreographers that we're pushing people too early, and this is why here in this company I let them quietly work throughout the year building material without necessarily always exposing the work to the full repertoire. It goes into the workshop season and if I think it can go into the repertoire, then I feed it in. Later I give people an opportunity to make work regularly for the main performances. It is such a big jump to suddenly go into our main repertoire; you then stand alongside established choreographers like Jiri Kylian, Merce Cunningham, Sue Davies or myself. These people have a craft which they have developed over decades. Every time I make something that's not good enough it hurts, but I'm philosophical and experienced enough to deal with it; you've got to be able to work quietly with integrity and develop the hard disciplines of structure and subject matter. There should be more opportunities for people to experiment

and not necessarily to show the work. I think budding choreographers need nurturing for longer. You've got to be better than we were 20 years ago because the standards are so much higher, the demands are so much greater. But you also have to learn to be extremely severe and disciplined with yourself.

Gill: *Who was advising you at an early stage?*

Christopher: The director of the company – it was Norman Morrice at the time – and colleagues. I was very alone, of course, because I was very young when I started, but I had been dancing for six years in a very varied repertoire. I was always very insecure about anything I ever did, but in the end there was also a perverseness. Sometimes you're right, sometimes not, but in the end it has to be your choice. I received a great deal of support from my directors at the time. I listened to people, took criticism, that's important. The other thing that's terribly important is that each choreographer should discover and define his own vocabulary.

Gill: *Don't you think that also takes time?*

Christopher: Absolutely. Therefore, you've got to be given the time and you've got to invest in the time personally. That's why I think when you've been in the business a bit longer you learn to observe and make some choices about what line you want to take, which influences. You always start off being influenced. Of course, that's the way it should be. Then you've gradually got to develop your own language. I work with all the languages I've learnt, from tap dancing, from musicals, theatre, very simple gestural movement through to all the classical and modern dance genres. All of this feeds into what I create, then I narrowly squeeze it down to a language for each particular piece. In the end, though, if there is a real choreographer in there, the talent will come out, whatever hurdles there are to overcome.

Jonathan Burrows
in conversation with Matteo Fargion

Jonathan Burrows in conversation with Matteo Fargion, August 1998

Matteo: *What was your starting point for your most recent piece, Things I Don't Know?*

Jonathan: Well, I started off by making a solo, because I felt it would be good to have a break from working across that gap between myself and another person, another dancer. I thought that I could make a leap sideways at that point if I worked on myself. In the previous piece that I made, *The Stop Quartet*, I had followed through certain ideas quite rigorously. When I came to make this solo I wanted to take the best of what I had learnt from that but also to have much larger elements of freedom for myself.

Matteo: *Can you describe your very first ideas?*

In a way it was quite a simple process: I decided that I would gather clusters of possible material and it was always 9 things - and I would use those 9 things until I'd had enough or finished with them or needed something else, and then I'd find another 9 things. I could do that at any point and I went on gathering these clusters until I felt like I had finished the piece. Another thing was that I had never really used entering and exiting as a way of building energy, and that became the other main element.

Matteo: *Did you find the material through improvisation?*

Jonathan: Eventually I did, but that was at a point when I felt that what I was doing needed to blossom again in a different way. But to start with I took a book of anatomy and traced curves and lines from the skeletal or muscle system, or I drew round parts of my own body to give me lines to start out with. That was one way but there were also much simpler methods: for instance 9 different balletic positions was one thing that eventually came in.

Matteo: *Then you would improvise to shape the material?*

Jonathan: Yes, so there was already a starting point to improvise with. In many ways it was more like I was improvising a rhythm than looking for physical material. I would do something, then I would video it and then I would learn it back again and edit it as I went along. This is a really laborious process, but it does work!

Matteo: *Did you pre-plan the structure of the piece, as you did in The Stop Quartet, or did you work more intuitively this time?*

Jonathan: I think that I had an idea of the durations just to get me started when I was still working on paper, in order to monitor what I was doing as I went along , but I can't actually remember.

Matteo: *Did you work with a metronome again?*

Jonathan: With *The Stop Quartet* I had worked with pulses from a metronome in order to upset the speed that I normally would move... to expand the natural speed of moving and encompass other speeds of moving. But with the solo what I decided was that rather than impose the pulse from the beginning, I would discover it as I went along. I would move at whatever speed I wanted to move, make a note of that speed and for the first 3 or 4 weeks of working I collected those speeds until eventually, in the second month of working, I kind of boiled it all down and came up with the pulse which seemed to be the pulse that I wanted to work with.

Matteo: *How long did it take you to make the solo?*

Jonathan: I think it took it took me 2 months, just working a couple of hours a day.

Matteo: *Why did you call it Things I Don't Know?*

Jonathan: Well, I think solos often tend to have the image of being about demonstrating what you can do, and I wanted to free myself from that. Calling it *Things I Don't Know* meant that I knew that I could also fail. I suppose because of that it turned out virtuosic. I think that had I set out to make it virtuosic I would have got lost.

Matteo: *What happened after the solo? What was the next part of the piece that you worked on?*

Jonathan: Well, I started working with Dana Fouras and Ragnhild Olsen on a trio, which I got briefly very excited about. Then what happened was that I received a letter from the composer Tom Johnson (whom I had worked with in the previous year). Tom is one of the first generation of American Minimalist composers and his work is very mathematical. He said he had been playing with an idea but it wasn't useful to him and thought it might be interesting to me: it was a kind of mathematical loop, basically a long sequence of numbers (or letters in this case). So I sent this off to Dana Fouras and asked her to do some homework - the sequence was in two parts and I suggested that she should learn the first and I would learn the second part. This was happening at the same time as we were trying to work on the trio, so Dana and I got together and tried it ...I actually just used some material from my solo and just applied it to this structure that he sent.

Matteo: *You assigned a different movement to each letter of Tom's sequence?*

Jonathan: Yes, and we videoed the result and it was much more interesting than the trio work. So we dumped the trio and then Tom's loop became the starting point for a duet for Ragnhild and Dana. But actually we're working on a trio again now, and I realised the other day that the best things about the old trio had resurfaced in the new. So it's funny, I do think those things you abandon are never wasted, the important things will come back when you need them.

Matteo: *How much did Dana and Ragnhild contribute to the piece? For instance I think you mentioned that you were imagining the material at only half the speed that it is now...*

Jonathan: After the solo it was quite difficult to step outside of the piece, and I realised that this was something that I had never really resolved and I was determined to find a way to stay really connected to what was happening whilst not actually being in it. I was also determined that there should be some elements of choice for them within what they were doing, to best use their skills. So in the first week of work, I presented them with all the drawings of body parts that I had used for my solo and gave them a pulse and various other parameters to work completely freely with. The funny thing was that they actually rejected all my parameters because they seemed to know exactly what to do! I think only two things that they did in that week made their way into the final piece but again it wasn't to say that that week was wasted because it influenced a lot of the decisions that we subsequently made about material. Once we started to work with Tom's loop a very interesting thing happened: we had started out doing it quite slowly, Dana and I, but when I handed it over to Dana and Ragnhild they very quickly started doing it at incredibly fast speeds and it was very exciting. Then we got to a point at which we had a choice as to whether we use this thing in a very 'Tom Johnson' way, in other words quite methodically, or accept it as a found object and do whatever we want with it.

Matteo: *You went for the freer option?*

Jonathan: Yes. We started to explore its properties in a very free way, we cut it up and reversed it and all sorts of things. I must say Tom has never seen the finished duet but he did say: "Oh well that's ok because it's probably much more interesting for it to be fuzzy logic!"

Matteo: *How do the 2 parts of the piece, the solo and the duet, relate to each other?*

Jonathan: Well I'm not sure... I have a few ideas about that, I mean one idea being that maybe they are two separate pieces, another idea being that I might make the solo into a duet with another man, but I don't know... I haven't finished with it yet.

Matteo: *So the piece has changed a lot from how you originally envisaged it. Your work generally seems to go through huge changes, even at the touring stage...*

Jonathan: The process isn't finished at the first performance. I have realised recently that so long as we're performing a piece, the process that you start when you first sit down with a piece of paper and write down your first idea continues, it never stops. In dance it doesn't ever seem to stop. I was reading recently this wonderful comment that Cunningham made about how one of the jobs of a dancer is to go on finding the difficulty in what they're doing, that if it gets too easy for them it dies, so they have to go on inventing the original awkwardness of it.

Matteo: *At which point did you start working with the music?*

Jonathan: Initially I didn't have enough money to commission a score so I persuaded Kevin Volans that we should take as a starting point the synthesizer version of a piece he had already written for me, for Ballet Frankfurt. This computer version sounded completely different from the live version, which was for percussion. So I would just put that tape on occasionally when I was working on the solo. When I had finished it I sent him a video (with the music) and Kevin found it too two dimensional. He later called me up and said he was writing another piece of music for it, which was pretty nerve-racking because I had a performance 2 weeks later! He sent me this other piece of music which was very beautiful but quite different.

Matteo: *Did you then have to change what you were doing?*

Jonathan: When I first danced with the new music I had great difficulty, I couldn't stay in the same place that I had been in with the other music, I was getting pulled into a whole different world which was dragging me down. Dana was rehearsing me and eventually she said: "You are fighting this music the whole way through and it's exhausting you, and it's exhausting to watch!" She suggested that I find three or four places where I would allow myself to enter into the emotional world of the music completely. This was a really intuitive leap! By building a map I could decide when to allow the music in, or when to be open but not allow the music in. I used to follow that map initially, now I have reached a point where I forget about that, I don't need it any more.

Matteo: *Do you think that your work survives in silence, that it doesn't need music?*

Jonathan: Well, it's important that you don't rely on your collaborators to save you, in other words your work has to be tough enough. But at the same time I think that sometimes what I'm doing can become almost too self sufficient, and not allow collaborators in. It's scary, but if you can let them in then there's the chance that the piece might go somewhere you hadn't expected, be bigger than you.

Matteo: *What's the thing you have most difficulty with when working?*

Jonathan: There are two things I suppose that are particularly difficult, and they're almost the opposite of each other. The first is that sometimes it takes a while for movement to enter right into a dancer's body, and in the meantime you can't tell whether it's working or not. On the other hand sometimes a movement in its first raw version can look wonderful, but then when the dancer becomes more familiar with it it can get smoothed down and begin to disappear. Perhaps that's what Cunningham meant when he talked about keeping it awkward. I think perhaps if things are complex enough to begin with, then even when your body gets used to what you're doing there will always something to challenge you.

Matteo: *Do dancers find it difficult working with you?*

Jonathan: As you can see dance can often be quite contradictory, and it's frustrating for dancers that the choreographer says one thing one day and then says something completely different the next. But actually those contradictions seem to be a really important part of the process. If for instance you say on the first day "Do it strongly", and then on the second "Do it passively", it may appear contradictory but actually the dancer needed to do it strongly first to discover one thing about it before they could move on to a more passive approach. I'm not sure why the medium is like that but it does seem to be. It takes an enormous amount of trust.

Siobhan Davies
in conversation with Gill Clarke

Siobhan Davies in conversation with Gill Clarke
June 1998

Gill: *We're going to focus on the piece titled Bank, but I was thinking that often it is something that's arisen from the previous piece that sets you off in the direction to the new piece, and wonder if might this be true of Bank?*

Siobhan
(Sue): Yes, when describing what I do in the studio to make a piece, of course, what I really want to do is to produce a good piece in its own and the dancers' and audience's terms. So that some of the things I might talk about now are very important to us as process, but the evidence of this work does not necessarily need to be clear by the time we reach the finished piece. The process is used as a key to get into another place and the getting into the other place is what one wants.

So the key is to enter into a larger realm of dance than the one I was in before, to get into a wider corridor, to get into a more exciting place, to break down the barriers that my lack of knowledge has had up until that point. So in *Affections*, the piece before *Bank* - one of the ways for me to manoeuvre into a more explicit area of dance for myself is how I choose the music, and this choice by its nature brings along a different set of questions and a different set of needs. So, therefore, choosing something like the Handel arias for *Affections* helps break down some of these barriers and enter new ground. The mezzo soprano is a very ample sound, and the songs are mostly structured ABA, even though I tried sometimes to break away from that structure, and each aria has a beginning, a middle and an end and a wholeness about it.

So immediately after making *Affections* I looked for a context to make *Bank*, and it couldn't be more different than to have Matteo Fargion's percussive piece already on an unusual instrument - amplified cardboard boxes - a piece that isn't sectionalised. Although each part of it is very particular, it moves across the landscape of sound and isn't a series of self-sufficient statements. There are paths from one section through into another for the 25 minutes or so of its duration.

Gill: *So do you find yourself listening to a lot of music with this sense of looking for something very different?*

Sue: Well, by answering the previous question as I just have, it suggests that the music is the leader and that's not true. The prime reason for going back into the studio or to make a piece for the theatre, is to try and make a better piece, in which dance is the foremost expression, and the companions that I use in order to help me do that are music and design.

So I am constantly listening to music, partly because I enjoy it and partly because it 'roughs me up' in a particular way, although a certain kind of movement or a certain kind of structure, or a certain kind of expression will be leading me towards a certain kind of music, so in that sense the dance comes first.

Gill: *The sense of companionship seems important because while it seems to me music is vitally important to you like many other choreographers it's not the thing that you search for and, having found, let dictate all your thinking about the movement. So even from the outset you're looking for a companion in your thinking about the piece as well as in the structuring or your moulding of its movement?*

Sue: Yes... the reason I use the word 'companion' is if I have good friends, I don't choose friends who agree with me, I don't choose friends whose lives structure me. I choose hopefully to have friends who I grow with, alongside, by being in conversation with them, by seeing them change over a period of time, by seeing myself change in their eyes over a period of time.

Gill: *So was that a pre-existing piece of music of Matteo Fargion's?*

Sue: The first 10 minutes were, which remained recorded in the final version, not live. And that was the springboard for writing the final piece.

Gill: *So in those early discussions with Matteo, there must have been points that you had to communicate somehow as to that "different place" you wanted to move into, in terms of movement or physical imagery?*

Sue: I think once I'd heard the first 10 minutes I knew that it was a very different sound world that he was, at that particular time, inhabiting. I could relax quickly into being curious about what he was going to do next rather than worrying about whether he was going to deal with *my* problems. So the most important thing is that I feel totally confident in him as a composer which I always had. He had found a sound world that fascinated him and was raring to go. But the point of commissioning a composer is that at the point I have commissioned them I have heard as much as I can of the music that they have written or recorded up until that point. Then once I've said "go" then I think they've got to go away and make the piece and I shouldn't interfere in what is their private, knowledgeable, passionate process. I should have chosen wisely in the first place.

Gill: *So then in terms of beginning to make the movement, you go into the studio with a blank page in the sense that you don't come in with movement that you demonstrate to the dancers. You want to make something _with_ them but what preparation have you done in your head and/or through to some physical sensation or picture of movement that prepares you for that first day? How tangible is that?*

Sue: Well, I wish I could make it sound a bit less abstract than it is going to sound. I think a lot about the kind of thrust, a mixture of the kind of movement direction I want myself and the dancers to move into. Now the movement   normally covers a similar area and interest,   but each time I re-approach it, it's a little bit different simply because of more knowledge, age, more experience or the mistakes that you've made in the past. So the over-riding thrust is to make quite sure that the performer, by the end of the process and leading into all the performances, has something very tangible to hold on to and to express in terms of movement and ideas. In order for that to be a very real physical experience then the movement has to start with an idea and it is, at first, in words only. It is in those first few seconds of rehearsal where I'm saying words not action, that you are beginning to give an image or a physical pathway through the body and/or a new geography of the entire body, a new alignment between various parts of the body. This is all to break down habits that we have as dancers. Dancers attune their bodies on a daily basis and after so many years' work that attunement can fall like a river running through earth. So water tends to run along a certain path, and in order to explore a fresh approach to movement, a new vitality in movement, you have to ask the body occasionally to re-work itself so that water runs through a different pathway.

So for early rehearsals, I have collected together some imagery, some thoughts on how to align the movements differently, some emotional ideas that I would like gradually to move through the piece. And I hopefully attain some structural ideas that the piece could gradually move towards once we have started building up the movement vocabulary. Now there are billions of ways of making movement, making pieces and to me the seeds that I'm going to plant are in those early movements that we make in the first two or three weeks of rehearsals, and my relationship with the dancer then is that I'm trying to come up with ideas which release the dancer from habitual movement, make them curious - yet again for God's sake, which is pretty extraordinary - about finding a slightly different approach to the movement, and then that seed literally begins to grow. If one's going to use this metaphor we have to make quite sure that the seed is planted in good soil and that we are adding ideas and we are giving confidence to that movement. This one seed might become several different ones that can be put together, or the first few ideas that started in day 1 have changed so much by day 6 that you've forgotten day 1's material, but you're already on a different level by the time you've got to day 6 material.

Gill: *You talked about ideas and emotions, even structure. I feel while it's clear that you come into rehearsal with all that, the strength of what you're doing is that where we begin from is actually very physical. You have a sense of those things in the back of your head which are going to colour the final piece but actually we're not starting from an idea that we are then illustrating but from a physical task or challenge or question.*

Sue: The whole idea of going right back to the beginning is the desire to make a better dance piece. So all the things I've described are the 'given' of my making a better dance piece, so I get into the studio and I have this backlog of desire, backlog of ideas unsolved, and then I move on.

Let's take *Bank* as a physical example. I arrive in the studio with a complex constantly changing rhythmical percussive piece on boxes. I arrive in the studio with a whole series of pattern books from patterns in textiles, patterns on china, patterns on the ground, calligraphy, from various different cultures: American Indian, Japanese, Chinese, African, Eskimo, Australian. And these were there to take the dancer and myself briefly out of the body in order to see an idea slightly abstracted - so that you're not having to explore everything internally all the time, which can get very frustrating as if you're trying to re-invent yourself constantly. So here we have an idea out of body, a series of very intricate patterns, some of them incredibly intricate. And one of the first things we did was choose one of the patterns, and then see what your foot does by describing that pattern on the floor. OK very shortly you worked out that it didn't do a great deal but at least you started putting that external idea internally into your feet. Then you slowly moved on, you could imprint the pattern through your entire body using the volume of your body, that you have width to your body, that you have depth to your body and what happens if your hips take one part of the pattern and your shoulders the other? Movement begins to start shifting into your body at a different level than it has already, much laughter is to be had throughout the studio as people turn round and aren't able to link certain things together - in particular the African patterns as they go very complicatedly in one direction and then sort of stop in mid-air. It was very pleasurable involvement.

So you then have a volume of movement in the body. You then try to think of passing through the pattern as if it was ahead of you like a wall, finding what happens to your body as you pass through that pattern and it comes out through your back, from front to back. You try to think of one pattern in your upper half and a different pattern in your lower half. You then try and work a pattern, your pattern, against somebody else's pattern and see where you can fit around each other. Now the big problem that I felt we came across immediately was that if you dealt with a floor pattern, your body action became less interesting and if you dealt with a pattern through the body you never moved anywhere because your whole body was involved with making the pattern. And the excitement was about how you spatially grabbed hold of something that might have been a calligraphic wiggle or a maze in an African textile, throw that out on the floor and try and fulfil that whilst at the same time doing quite complex body action. So now you're early on in the rehearsal process and you have actually got lots of movement. It was incredibly exciting to be in those rehearsals and see the pleasure in all the performers as they thought "Oh I have not explored this path before."

The next hurdle you have to go through is you've discovered all these new methods of making either a pattern pass through your body or in putting a pattern out into space or you putting your pattern across somebody else and it's a reasonably abstract calligraphic idea in space. Very beautiful - but now, and this is where my job becomes a much larger part than only worrying about the individual movement, how do you structure this whole thing so that the eye of any individual member of the audience is led through into this country which is telling you about something highly humane but is using these parameters in which to deal with it? And by structuring the entire piece, and I wish I could be clearer about this, you enter into this different country and suddenly these people whose world has, up until that point, been pattern based, you suddenly see that one person's enforced pattern is making somebody else's liberated. So therefore, you begin to get into the ideas of people who keep to a pattern and people who allow themselves a freer range to move into in an emotional way. You see the idea of travelling across the stage in a different way. Of one person going somewhere and being interfered with by another person and what happens with that interference by a certain rhythm being built up over a period of time and being irritated, offset or even enjoyed by somebody else.

Gill: *And do those kind of ideas develop as you see the material taking shape? Are they partly in your head already from having listened to the music?*

Sue: They weren't there from listening to the music, they were there from starting the patterns idea to begin with. And yes, I knew that the abstract idea of asking dancers to look at pattern structures should, if we really tried to keep focused, lead us to these far more human discussions about who, where and when.

Gill: *I can remember going back several times over the structure of the very beginning of the piece. It seemed very important, having made this thing that was highly complex, how you let the audience into it, even more maybe than many other pieces. Do you have recollections about that?*

Sue: Yes we'd made a fair amount of movement, hadn't we, and then I had to start making the piece.

Gill: *Which doesn't necessarily always happen from A-Z.*

Sue: Absolutely. And just as a start I had a very lovely African design of a path, a snake and a man, just very flatly on one piece of paper, parchment I think it was. So I just used that as a blueprint to see where it would get us. Paul Old on stage right took the figure of the man, Sarah Warsop in the middle took the sort of snakelike figure and you and Deborah Saxon eventually took the pathlike figure. The audience doesn't have to know these details at all, but I had to start with a strong image and a strong image that was movement related. You can have an image until you're blue in the face but if it isn't movement related it doesn't help. Or it doesn't help me. So I placed Paul on one side of the stage doing a repeated action moving up and down. In the middle of the stage I had something that immediately took on a very different movement quality from what had happened to Sarah's right and then I had quite an obsessive pattern happening to stage left. So I set those three things up straight away, all with their own movement ideas, all visually clear. Then in order to make it more interesting I began to scratch from stage right interferences from two other men who gradually, rhythmically, get involved spatially with Paul and become a trio. The woman in the middle is left reasonably still. She had lots of movement to begin with, and I pared that down and pared it down because by her stillness she caused an ongoing build-up of presence that became more and more powerful, and then I had to make you and Deborah more and more intense at the side in order to make quite sure that that pattern was to do with one person infringing on somebody else's space in a reasonably obsessive but utterly clear way. In fact, you never get in each other's way but you're ridiculously close and I think that tension comes across to the audience. So this took, as you say, a lot of time to pare down but in one fell swoop you have an image, movement ideas and movement qualities clearly stated. And emotional ideas, humane ideas at the same time.

So then we had a solo for Sarah which had some extraordinary animal gestures in it because a lot of the patterns which were built particularly from medieval patterning had intricate spirals in the middle but ended up with a paw or a snake's head or something else at the side. So that was again using visual movement ideas. We then had you sweep across the stage in very open arcs as if you could wipe out what had gone before but you were left with the memory of it, and then more complex lines of pattern coming in from stage right, built partially on the men's scratching ideas but opened out a bit more, and after that you swept across the stage again with your eraser. We still had a memory of it but you'd cleaned the idea away in order to be refreshed for the next part. Now with hindsight it was right up until there, but it took a lot of doing, a lot of re-adjusting, getting rid of too much material. It's a dilemma with any art form - you're dying to use the tools that you've got, which in our case is a dancer dancing. You get very interesting dance material, but so what if you're not really doing anything with it. So sometimes you have to take some of the excellent material away in order to make quite sure that what you remain with is really seen.

Gill: *One characteristic of the piece is that it is not only individual movements or phrases that you see again or from a different perspective, but also whole sections repeat. It feels as though that was one way of allowing something to actually be very complex and yet register with an audience. By seeing it a second time one gains a certain familiarity.*

Sue: This is the fascinating thing about being 30 years into watching material because what I see and what you see reasonably rapidly, for an audience whose knowledge of dance is not a daily experience there's no reason why they should see that. However, my absolute prime commitment and concern is to turn round and make the best possible piece, all that we are capable of seeing, and therefore, its richness and its complexities are of interest to me in the same way as any other creative artist. But with music you can go back to it again and again and the problem with dance is that it lives very much in the present, and even with video and film and notation I think one should never deny that its glory is in the moment. But in order to give it value historically, and to make quite sure that people are able to even think in terms of contemporary dance having a true value, how do we give it the weight and importance it deserves so that at least the memory of it is that it was complex and real when it existed?

And then on the opposite side I have the audience, who very much want to see dance in its complexity; they've gone to the cinema, they've read books, they've listened to music, they don't want to be let down by over-simplicity but they do want to respond to what they've seen. So how to structure something so that the audience can say "Yes I've seen that before, and so there's a moment of pleasure of recognition, now I can see it again, I can feel more part of it. I feel more established in my relationship to the material", or "Yes I've seen it again but why does it look different?" and you suddenly realise that you're seeing it from another angle. Or "Yes it looks different again, different style, different dancer."

Gill: *A running joke within the company is that often you will say "This is going to be simple" or "this needs to be simple" and it ends up extraordinarily complicated. Or this piece is going to be simple whereas the last one was extraordinarily complicated and actually they get more and more complex. So what is your desire for simplicity?*

Sue: I suppose I'd absolutely adore to produce a piece of movement that was complex enough to be fully involving, but that had the simplicity to be utterly memorable, and I'm thinking of Bach's *Art of the Fugue*. And there you have one phrase and then its dealt with from every perspective, superbly intelligent, utterly riveting and totally beautiful. And I'm not going to do it but in the back of my head is just the sheer extraordinariness of the possibility that at one point, even briefly in one part of a piece, I might just do that.

Gill: *I don't know that one should have to choose between these two, but do you think it is more of a challenge than say having the impact of an extraordinary piece by Stravinsky the first time it was ever heard?*

Sue: Oh *Rite of Spring?* I just think it's something I lean towards and probably won't do and probably I think in most of my pieces and to some extent in my life, I deal with opposites all the time. You know, I'm one person trying to be another, I'm producing a piece of movement that wants to be something else. But actually it's terribly healthy for what I do because instead of pouring over the edge into somewhere and not ever having a counterbalance – the counterbalance, the fight, the mixture of indecision at a certain point and then suddenly decision – is how I think I work better.

Gill: *Which is partly the companionship with the other elements of the piece also? So talk about the design a little. At what stage in your thinking do discussions begin and how much is that also a companion in the same way as the music?*

Sue: I think every designer I've worked with, and it's mostly been David Buckland, has been very aware that he comes in quite often last in the equation and that's partly because he knows fundamentally that I need space and time to dance in.

Gill: *So am I right in saying that he's stimulated by your thinking about the piece, isn't he, rather than the movement you've made?*

Sue: Yes, it's the thinking not the movement. So he knew the music for **Bank,** he knew the idea about patterns from before rehearsals but also during rehearsals; he knew in this instance that he wanted to stand back and make the decision later in the piece because he could see how complex the material was going to be, and he liked the ideas we spoke about of energy being forced along a particular pathway. He had, in fact, photographed Frank Whittle before he died for the National Portrait Gallery and having been fascinated by engineering and his idea of the jet engine which forced energy through a particular path, I think that's what led him towards putting that on the backcloth. Again it's also a terribly humane shape. I mean lots of people thought it was parts of the insides of a person and I think he enjoyed that ambiguity very much. We knew that by painting the picture with some paint substance that of would show up in some lights and not in other lights, it would have a slight three dimensional quality and some bits would vanish and some bits would come forward like memory - remembering something when it was there and then forgetting it because it wasn't and then remembering because it turns up again.

The word 'memory' means quite a lot to me as well. That's also how you structure a piece and how you involve the audience so that by the end of the piece there will be certain places which you have memorised well, and there'll be certain parts that won't be in your front brain thinking but will be in your back brain because you have seen them turn up in certain guises. Our lives are, I think, so much to do with what we remember and what we forget: who you are, when you are and where you are and I think all those things are what dance both explicitly and abstractly deals with in an extraordinary way. It means that by the end of the dance performance, if it has worked well, you can have gone through an entire experience without it being explicit and attached to a story, but essentially you will have gone down, I feel, a very human path using these different parts of your sensibility, your intelligence and your imagination.

Gill: *So tell me if this is completely wrong. I remember having a sense when we'd finished the piece, near to performance, that you suddenly weren't sure about how this would communicate with an audience. I almost felt as though you were happy with it for what it was, but concerned that it might not communicate humanly enough, would it be too abstract in one sense? Would it have remained too much as movement and pattern?*

Sue: You're absolutely right. I did feel that very strongly. I felt what I'd done, which I was very pleased with, was I'd really gone the whole course structurally and with the kind of movement we'd all made, and that I'd been quite a hard taskmaster on all of you in terms of the quality of movement which was wonderful from everybody. Everybody had been energised by the ideas and I was very terrified that it was slightly bereft, that I hadn't quite managed to get that human endeavour through it. And I thought it was a lot to do with the endeavour of searching, having limitations, being liberated from those limitations. All those kind of things. I thought it was clear and then I finished the piece, I looked at it in the studio and I was worried it wasn't there. In other words the search for a sort of movement perfection and structural perfection had, in fact, closed the door on something else. But I don't think I tinkered with it at that point. I thought, no I've done it, this is the piece, I've done it.

Gill: *I think what drew that to my attention was that you talked to us about the performance of it in a way that usually you don't.*

Sue: I had given myself and I had given you very real practical problems. For instance, we'd had those very quick sections of 5 people, where you were wrapping yourselves around each other at a very speedy level. When it went wrong there would quite often be a break-out of laughter and an immediate human response to the situation. What I wanted was to make quite sure that endeavouring to do the movement was a human response in itself and that, therefore, the liveliness with which you did that and the sense of daredevilry: am I going to move for you or not, yes I am, or another time no I'm not you're going to have to go round... the decisions that we'd made had to be re-invented and re-shown. And once we got back onto that again it became much wittier. I needn't have worried because we did the first night and I was astounded by the audience reaction. They did very quickly turn round and talk about its wit, speed, human qualities and it did seem to start from somewhere and definitely go the whole hog somewhere else and it was satisfying to watch. And that gave me enormous pleasure.

Gill: *Is that sometimes a hard transition to make? From seeing something very very close in the studio to imagining it on the stage?*

Sue: It's brutal. In the early days of this company our first programme was successful. And then I started to make pieces in which I was so involved with the work in the studio that, I know it sounds silly, I did think about what they would look on stage but I didn't think well enough. I learnt that from day one those first seeds of movement eventually are going to have to be seen and, therefore, I try and give information about how that work has to be seen. I quite often say to dancers, this movement can't be seen, it may be a very good strong emotional intelligent idea in your head, but if we can't demonstrate it it's not going to work. And I talk a lot about how the movement is going to be demonstrated beyond the immediate moment of making it and when the sets start coming into play then I begin to feel as if the piece has two lives. It has its practical life that is being made and the other life, which is eventually the finished piece. There are still shocks, because you go on stage and most of the movement can be seen, but in juxtaposition to light and sound and set there are still the threats, the ever-constant threats of one thing dominating more than the other. And then you have a very short period of time on stage in which to make very brutal decisions about what is best for the entire piece. So in the latest piece *Eighty-Eight* David had made a beautiful set, we had seen mock-ups of it and discussed it. We had made decisions with the production manager, everybody had been involved but, in fact, when it went up on stage, these very beautiful white pillows with the indentations of dancers' heads on them couldn't be there because of their very whiteness and luminosity and strength.

Gill: *Which leads me on to... Am I right in thinking that quite often the place you arrive at... of course it has a connection to the place you began but..*

Sue: But the whole point is that you've got to a place that you haven't been in before. The whole point is that however dreadful I am or how good, that somehow I have made a bigger place for dance at that moment than I ever realised before, and if I knew I was going to do that to begin with, what's the point in doing it. We're not talking about enormous, enormous changes it just means the landscape is larger.

Gill: *I read an interview in the paper yesterday with novelist Arunhati Roy (The God of Small Things) and the interviewer was mentioning her love of the play with language, and she said that language was only the messenger and that what was important was the thought. What most pleases you in an audience response to a piece? What do you feel you want them to take away with them? I suppose in a narrow sense what do you feel you are communicating?*

Sue: I wish I could be a little more specific. Let me try. It's that there is knowledge about being human. Our daily lives are limited to what we have to achieve in that day, quite often. The small but terribly vitally important things of getting up, walking, working, feeding, the pragmatic parts of one's life, and there are the other parts of one's life that actually you have to get involved with in order to understand what kind of emotional areas you want to move into, what kind of partnerships you want to have with friends and loved ones and children and parents. What kind of places you want to go and visit. One thing that I think all the arts do for you is they take you to a place that you haven't been before. Now in music orally you are given information through your ears, nothing to do with words. It opens up your ears to a combination of sounds, rhythms, worlds, it completely expands your sense of hearing and involves new emotional perspectives. Through your ears you are somewhere else. In the same way, the eyes can recognise information given by the visual arts, but that information can be intellectually and emotionally juggled with, clear statements of objectives, or real new visual dilemmas for eyes, head and heart to adjust to. In literature you are much more likely, through our close understanding of words, to be involved in the story of the action. But if you take any Shakespeare play, it's not the story, it's not **Romeo and Juliet**, it is that extraordinary use of words which describes love and passion and placement and dilemma in a very, very particular way. So finally I get to speaking about dance, in which we don't have a literary plan. We have a physical part of the body opened up a little bit further, revealing human dilemmas, problems and joys. As I said before, we deal with who, when and where, how close you are to someone, how you are placed in any particular field of activity, when you do something, what energy level you do it with, what passion you do it with; speed, timing, grace, slowness, memory, all those things can be dealt with by dance in a non-linear but unbelievably revealing way, so if any member of the audience turns round and says to me "I'm not quite sure if I could speak to you about the piece, but I feel as if I've just been in a different place and I'm going to go away and think about it" that is wonderful, and I don't want to sound vain, but one hopes that their landscape is larger.

Gill: *So, in the time between making pieces you go to a lot of art exhibitions, you go to theatre, you read a lot; could you say a little about what sensibility you're taking to those things, how they might inform your thinking, whether you ever make translations to dance when you are experiencing those other art forms?*

Sue: Not in a clear way. Within the last few months I saw a Tom Stoppard play and a Harold Pinter set of plays, so in one there was an incredibly dense use of language, you had to be on your toes to listen to every single moment and idea. Then I went to the Harold Pinter play and the words are not the important part, it's the silences, it's what isn't said that you hear, I don't know how he does it. Well that polarisation was fantastic because it suddenly gives me the most enormous range to work within. There is no one way of giving information. I'll go to a minimalist art event in which a very few lines can express or not express a great deal. David came back from India with the most incredible visual images in which ancient Indians put the most enormous amount of information about their sexuality, their lives, the richness of their lives, what they wore, what they ate, what the plants and trees were like, the vegetation: all in, you know, one stone leaf. There are a billion ways of giving or taking information; the dilemma for an artist is to choose the medium and then use that medium for what it's good at. We don't want to say dance is film or dance is literature. But movement, the human being moving, scratches away at a very different part of ourselves and gives information in a different way.

Gill: *Do you think dance is restricted? I mean it's a little bit like Renaissance Madonnas, we accept that form as a norm and then enjoy the different ways that it is painted. In dance we have become accustomed to seeing a love story of some kind or another, and so then maybe that's communicating on a very direct level to an audience, meanwhile they might be enjoying how it is differently coloured this time. Obviously you haven't chosen the narrative route so you feel there's something about the medium itself, that it doesn't need that mould to pour itself into?*

Sue: I don't think it does at all, and again I look at the other art forms; music probably started with songs. I was just thinking of the medieval era of song in which love or religion was sung about, and it was sung with the most incredibly simple rhythms behind it and those rhythms gradually became more complicated and the subject matter became more complicated. Dance has the ability, again like other art forms, to move between the abstract and the figurative - I think that's a brilliant range that you can work with, and you don't have to be one or the other. I think within one piece you can deal with how ten people are structured on stage, their rhythmic patterns, their negotiations of making marks on stage, and five seconds later you can deal with a very intimate moment between one or two people. Now, having had that range I think people get a little bit worried that if it gets too abstract it's not dealing with the main human subject, which is who loves who? And if you're not careful the art form is divided between those two polarisations. What I am saying is there's this incredible world in between, in which there are various forms of companionship, relationship, ability to be with one person and another person without there ever being any communication at all, to many different ways of patterning on stage, of structuring something on stage, of making a mark. I think I should be contemporary, I should be dealing with what we know now as contemporary people, but having said that I think so much is possible. The limitations are not the art forms. It's the practitioners and very understandably the people who are coming to see it who dictate the fashion of the day. There is a lot of talk about making the arts more accessible. But this is interpreted to mean access to the ordinary part of the imagination, whereas in fact the arts can be accessing the parts we don't reach on a daily basis, the stranger places.

If we make movement too literal and it becomes gesture, then the gesture dominates the action and the play of our intelligence and imagination, which doesn't seem a very good use of what should be a far reaching offer. Most of us would agree that our lives, the use of our life, intelligence and imagination is more limited than we know we are capable of. Then for heaven's sake let the artist use his skill to point out some of the expanses that are within us. We need to enable some people to refine certain skills, to have the time and commitment and then give us access to their particular quest.

Gill: *Yes, because we don't quibble if somebody is incredibly knowledgeable about our computer. What we do is ask them for help and information. So why do we quibble with an artist who has explored form over a lifetime and wishes to communicate that knowledge? After all what lives on in history is a country's culture and its battles!*

Sue: It does seem odd not to give artists the chance to explore the breadth of their form - but let's drop the battles!

Stuart Hopps
The Making of Nora:
A personal choreographic approach

THE MAKING OF NORA:
A personal choreographic approach
Stuart Hopps
May 1998

To work on a musical which has never before been staged is an enormously challenging undertaking. I have worked on such a brand new project only once before in my life, and it nearly saw an end to my career. I refer to the debacle with Jean Seberg at the National Theatre in 1983.

In his book *The National,* Simon Callow tries to explain how it was possible for the potential hit of the three workshop performances

"a dazzling showing, tightly and wittily choreographed by Stuart Hopps..."

to disintegrate into the disastrous flop it was to become six months later. Demoralised by the egotistical and destructive forces of the American authors, the book writer, the lyricist and in particular the composer Marvin Hamlisch, as well as by my own degree of self-made paranoia, I asked Peter Hall to release me from my contract some five weeks into the rehearsal period. Surrounded by such collaborators, and affected by what I felt at the time to be the weakness of the director, I found I simply could not function in the capacity of choreographer. Such was the negative impact of that experience that it took me several years to recover my confidence and to start choreographing again.

It is hardly surprising, therefore, that I responded to the invitation to choreograph the new American musical *The Betrayal of Nora Blake* with a modicum of caution. It is fairly true to say that in the commercial sector, the stimulus to create a new work can occur as a result of a telephone call from a director. Agents rarely provide regular employment for a jobbing choreographer, but they can ensure that your name is known, that terms and conditions are properly negotiated, and that any problems of employment are dealt with if they arise. Personally I have remained with the same agent since I left Scottish Ballet to go freelance in the late seventies, and that is an indication of how mutually beneficial our relationship has been. In the case of this new musical, *Nora Blake,* the call came from the actor Nicholas Grace in the spring of 1998 when I was directing Mozart's *Idomeneo* for the Norwegian National Opera in Oslo.

I had worked with Nicholas Grace before in productions of *Candide* and *H.M.S. Pinafore,* he as an actor and I as choreographer, and so he was already familiar with my movement style and working methods. Now he planned to work in the capacity of director, and his engagement and enthusiasm for the project was so communicated to me long distance, that I immediately suggested that he should send the script and the score. It was to be an enormously creative and rewarding collaboration.

For several days I read and re-read the script, listening endlessly to the tapes and studying the sheet music, before I made my decision. I have been sent scripts before and rejected them on the grounds that they lacked clarity, economy, sound structure, novelty and most importantly for me, wit. On my return to London, Nicholas invited me to lunch to persuade me to join him in this venture. In truth I needed no persuasion: I was excited by the originality of the idea, the freshness of the music, and the notion of working on a pastiche piece which parodied the Hollywood film noir style of the Forties. Somewhere deep inside me I know how to do this kind of work, I feel it my bones almost. I trust my own judgement and taste, and instinctively understand the referential choice of the movement style of the period. Of course, research is also essential; I need the confirmation which will enable me to realise the gestural language of the choreography.

The Betrayal of Nora Blake is the work of one man, John Meyer. The book, lyrics and music were all his, and in the world of music theatre, a command in all three areas is a rather unusual situation. Most current hit shows in the West End are the result of collaboration between several talents, composer, lyricist and book writer; here John is pretty unique. Lengthy discussions with Nick Grace preceded John's arrival from New York but not before my agent had discussed contractual terms with Cole Kitchenn, the British producers. My first meeting with Nick was on March 27th, final casting was achieved by 10th April, and preparation days with the author, director, producer and musical supervisor all took place prior to rehearsals commencing on Monday 20th April.

Nick and I spent several days together working through the score and script as it then existed prior to that first day of rehearsal. Playing each character in turn, we read through the dialogue which proceeded each song, then listened to the taped version of the vocal score. It was important to agree to the kind of physical setting required, or a particular use of space, or how rhythmic, energetic or contained the physical language should be. I had strong ideas for the staging and needed to talk these through. I felt that right from the opening number "Amnesia", the audience needed to know that they were watching a parody and that exaggerated use of shoulders, hips and arms, redolent of the Forties, should pervade the comic use of gesture and be performed with utter seriousness. It was also important that when the screens develop a life of their own at the top of the opening song they signal the humour that will flow throughout the evening.

I was also concerned with what I perceived to be faults in the structure. I suggested that both sisters have a song together, that "A Man in My Life" be reconstructed as a duet, and that the Act One Finale be simplified. In order that an antiphonal effect be achieved, the two songs "Schmuck" and "Doing to Nora" would have to be rearranged to avoid cacophony. Nicholas Grace and I were in total agreement and joined forces to influence the author to make these changes.

The show tells the story of twin sisters Nora and Laura Blake, both fashion designers, and the demise of the man in their lives, Spencer Wylie. The tale is told through a series of flash-backs, and transitions were effected by Nick's idea for the use of the two screens on wheels, which provided the device for scenes flowing one into the other and stimulated what later became known as my "screen ballet".

We spent several weeks casting. Nick insisted that I be involved in the selection process, and this was appreciated as in my experience it is not always the case that the director includes the wishes of the choreographer at this stage. Actors read from the script, sang one, sometimes two songs, a ballad and an up-tempo number, then if I had not seen them professionally and was unfamiliar with their movement capability I asked them to work with me. As I warmed them up, I tried to identify how strong their sense of rhythm was, and to test co-ordination I took them through a sequence featuring weight transference and directional change. Movement choices in the upper body and arms identified whether or not they would be able to pick up a sense of Forties' style.

The constraints of a low budget musical can be considerable. Apart from low wages, and set and costumes made on a shoe string, the rehearsal period can be brief and the size of the auditorium small. However, our American producer Bobbie Horowitz provided the resources for four weeks' rehearsal which was more generous than anticipated. Still, the "get-in" to the Jermyn Street Theatre was tight. We started the technical rehearsal at 2.00pm on a Monday afternoon and had only three sessions before the dress rehearsal on Tuesday afternoon followed by the first public preview the same evening at 7.45pm. I knew it was imperative to have entrances, exits, the spacing and placing of each musical number and the manipulation of moving screens which were crucial to this piece, all absolutely effective before we left the rehearsal room, since there was to be so little time once we got in to our small theatre. And I mean small; the stage is twenty feet wide by eleven feet deep, to take scenery, cast and band; it seats seventy.

Fortunately, my Half Moon Theatre days stood me in good stead. Director, cast, producers and even critics were surprised at what could be achieved in such a small area. I sensed the importance of the diagonal axis within the spatial limitation, thus providing volume and altering stage front on to the diagonal. I'm told that use of space is one of my strong points; I have to work harder at other things, but more of that later.

My official billing reads "Musical Staging by..." and the credit appears directly below that of the director, which is not always the case in poster advertisements for other shows. As the job description implies, I am responsible for what happens on stage from the moment the band strikes up, though this does not always include under-scoring during scenes. The choreographer's role here comprises the creation of all that which may be clearly recognisable as dance, together with controlling or manipulating the way in which the actors interact on stage. Inventive staging is no less difficult than complicated dance routines, and requires an understanding of a whole range of choreographic skills. Personally I place emphasis on spatial invention, surprising use of gesture, unexpected rhythmic patterns, and movement choices which develop character, theme and plot.

The Betrayal of Nora Blake has a cast of six actors and no less than fourteen musical numbers to set, some requiring danced sequences, and all inhabiting the same period feel of the Forties. We kept an extensive collection of books on Forties style and fashion in the rehearsal room. These, together with videos of Forties Hollywood movies and the daily warm-up, helped the cast acquire a common style. "Opening out the numbers", a term I heard Gillian Lynne describe brilliantly at a lecture last year, is the method of staging we used in rehearsal. I like to think of this as the 'Mount Everest' aspect of the work, consisting as it does of mapping out the material which already exists in score form.

This mapping often results in the addition of introductory music or the repetition of a chorus, adding an extra verse or devising a dance break. It can also include the editing or elimination of existing material. The intent here is that all development and amplification must serve the plot, further the action and/or deepen characterisation. For example, the addition of an 'apache style' dance break in "A Clever Girl Like You" served to demonstrate the schizophrenic side of the character Jeffrey Conte's murderous personality. Similarly the addition of a dance break in "Fishnet and Chicken Bones" served to heighten the fantasy element in that ridiculously over-the-top fashion show production number. This work requires an understanding of musical form and the structure of each section; the choreographer should attempt to illuminate a musical number, finding an appropriate balance between dance/movement and music without destroying it with over-elaborate staging or redundant dance interludes.

I use improvisation quite rarely when working on musicals, and although I encouraged the cast to contribute, we did not use improvisational techniques for either scenes or songs in this production. When working in opera, the sessions allocated with the chorus are usually so few that I find I cannot afford the luxury to work this way. Once familiar with the score so that I can sing and hum the tunes, I start preparing material at home. Inhabiting the characters' personalities and understanding the intention of scene and song, the movement begins to flow out of my body. I edit and clarify and check that my timing matches the structure of the music. I go through it with an assistant, (in this case with Alison Golding, whom I taught as a student at the Laban Centre in the eighties) as I know how the movement feels, but through her I can see what it looks like. I chose Alison because she has experience of working as a choreographer in musical theatre. She is a good communicator, knows how to get the best out of actors, is inventive and is a loyal colleague. I encourage assistants to feel that they are part of the process, contributing ideas and "feeding" steps. Alison has worked with on a number of projects, including the film *Amy Foster.*

On day one, I start at the beginning and work systematically through the show. Having the author and the American producer in the rehearsal room during this time proved challenging and Bobbie and John were with us for the entire first week. We felt it was an intrusion into the rehearsal process and this was discussed after a few days at a company meeting. It was like having parents at a teenage party. Understandably they were protective of a piece of work that had taken five years to evolve, but it was equally inhibiting to have them there. It was important to listen to John's reactions as each of the numbers neared completion, but it was equally important for me to hold my ground and sustain my conceptual ideas - I had learnt that hard lesson on *Jean Seberg*. Indeed, as I write this I can hear my mantra "...well, this is just the first draft, John..."

A typical rehearsal day started with a physical and vocal warm-up at 10.15am. It has been many years since I taught class, as in larger productions I usually ask my assistant to do that - but on this occasion I threw self and body into it enthusiastically. Some of the cast were older, and it was important to set a good example. I have also learnt that it is important to let the movement come from my own body, however badly I demonstrate. I inhabit the movement and therefore understand it and can communicate its meaning; after all, it emerges as my response to both the idea and the music, equally an intellectual and a physical choice.

Before rehearsals began I had already prepared a section of the most challenging dance section of "Fishnet and Chicken Bones", and from the second day of rehearsals this sequence was incorporated into the warm-up. I realised that we would not get to the big production number until well into the second week of rehearsal, but it was important to start teaching the material as early as possible, even if I then changed my mind and didn't use any of it. The function of this complicated sequence was to reveal the cast in a moment of bravura dexterity, demanding rhythmic precision and accurate co-ordination at speed, and I knew it would take the actors some time to get the sequence into their bodies. This was a gamble that paid off; all the material was used, and we added and built upon it each day; by the time we staged the number, the whole cast had familiarised themselves with the most difficult section. Alison, who could only join us after midday, watched the actors increase in confidence and dexterity, and was always there to take individuals aside, and to review what had been added each day.

Nicholas Grace was present for all the staging rehearsals unless he was at a production or publicity meeting, or working with an actor not involved in the particular section. My usual process here was to put the number on its feet as a first draft, then to consult with Nick, make changes where required and then move on to the next section. In other productions directors leave you completely on your own, while others interfere before you have the chance to settle on a first version.

Whenever a number was 'opened out', John and Nick were present together with the invaluable Hubert 'Tex' Arnold, our musical supervisor and arranger. Tex is something of a genius, able to transpose immediately and to improvise within John's musical framework so that a structure can be established and then the music composed. He was also responsible for the orchestration, which is particularly important for the choreographer of a musical in terms of the dance breaks, the introductions and musical endings. Tex's support and understanding was of vital importance during this process, and he played a significant role in realising the choreographic ideas in musical terms.

Although the cast of **Nora** always felt that they could contribute, and this created a healthy working atmosphere, it has to be said that in such an intense process there can only be one chief. However much I can influence decision-making, the director has the final veto. If as a choreographer you cannot function in this way - and it is true that in ballet and contemporary dance the choreographer has more autonomy - then it is best to avoid work in the theatre, opera, film or television!

I like to develop a strong point of view for each number, and to know what my objectives are. If these two elements are not in place, I find it hard to choreograph. The most challenging aspect of the work is in matching the text and music to the third element, the choreography: that's the hardest part for me. I keep a hidden check-list at the centre of my third eye: counterpoint and juxtapose; sometimes let the dance be the melody; never illustrate, unless for comic underpinning; avoid redundant decoration; and never eclipse the existing meaning. I like to leave room for inspiration on the floor in the moment.

In this musical, I knew that the number to introduce the wicked twin, "Not My Colour", had to be modelled on a strip-tease, but I worked out the actual sequences in the rehearsal. I enjoyed playing the vamp, and sensed that Issy van Randwyck, the actress playing the role, would too. Claire Moore who played the good twin was equally keen to extend her movement range and inhabit the style of the Forties, and we had great fun exploring the exaggerated style of gesture heavily laced in Forties' nostalgia in her opening number "Amnesia". Andrew C Wadsworth, an actor who has been in many West End shows, played Spencer Wylie, and proved to be endlessly inventive and generous in his contribution to the totality of what was being made. The entire cast on this occasion was exceptionally ego-free, supportive of one another (even when tiredness hit) and all were able to work together for the good of the piece - a refreshing contrast to other circumstances.

Movement images are a curious phenomena; I am not always sure of their provenance but I remember being very excited when I at last resolved "Let Her Burn". This number had required a lot of 'opening out'; suddenly it began to fall into place, and just as we were nearing completion, a circle of flame came into my mind's eye, providing me with the final movement image. Endings are notoriously difficult for all choreographers; finding a real resolution, as opposed to tacking something on to the end, is something that does not necessarily happen frequently. I'm not sure where my ending came from that day, but I remember going home feeling really inspired, and happy in the knowledge that the choreographic gods were still with me.

The Finale proved the most difficult to map out, but our invaluable musical supervisor Tex re-allocated the sung parts with the permission of the author, so that I could chart what I felt had to be the final statement. This section looks so simple now when I watch the show, but in retrospect it was the most difficult to realise.

Very few numbers had to be altered. "A Clever Girl Like You" had a dance break which had to be re-adapted to suit the actor and satisfy me, and after the show had opened I reinforced the final eight-bar phrase of Act 1 Finale with Nick's approval, to make greater impact prior to the interval.

I started choreographing in 1969 when I returned from the USA after studying dance composition with the late Bessie Schoenberg. Over the years, I have enjoyed the high points and relegated the failures to the realm of experience. But it is only when the work comes face to face with an audience that I know whether or not I have a hit; I cannot ascertain this at the last run through or even at the dress rehearsal. *An Clo Mor,* for Scottish Ballet, *The Oresteia* at The National Theatre, *Pal Joey* at the Half Moon Theatre, *The Cunning Little Vixen* at the Royal Opera House, *Carmen Jones* at the Old Vic... these were some of the successes... and now *The Betrayal of Nora Blake.* It is an inspiring feeling when the hard work of the collaborative process emerges as a glorious celebration, and when you have had the privilege to be a part of it.

Shobana Jeyasingh
in interview with Sanjoy Roy

Interview with Shobana Jeyasingh by Sanjoy Roy
May 1998

Shobana Jeyasingh trained in the classical Indian dance style Bharata Natyam, and began experimenting with this particular dance language in her choreography. Over the past decade of work, she has enriched this base with everyday and gestural movements, as well as drawing on the various movement skills of her dancers. Her current company of six women all have a training in Bharata Natyam, but also encompass skills in the martial arts kalari and chhau, and in ballet.

Intimacies of a Third Order is Jeyasingh's latest work, premiered in February 1998, with music by Michael Gordon, set by Madeleine Morris, and costumes by Ursula Bombshell.

Starting points

In an earlier conversation Jeyasingh mentioned that after finishing one piece, the beginnings of the next often seem 'just around the corner'. I asked if the seeds for *Intimacies* appeared in her previous piece, *Palimpsest.*

"I think it started off with the set. For *Palimpsest* I'd had a conversation with the designer, Keith Khan, about not using the centre of the stage, about using the edges. That interest arose from a conversation with [cultural critic] Homi Bhabha, about the idea of borders and margins – about capturing in dance the experience of being a border animal. So we thought about the edges of the stage space, the stage as a metaphor for the everyday. And one of the first things I thought about in *Intimacies* was about using the edge. The set we came up with, by Madeleine Morris, really intruded upon the stage space, shifted its centre – it was very busy on one side of the stage, leaving the other side empty."

But the starting point wasn't just about being 'on the edge' in a physical or in a social sense, but also of the emotional experience. Jeyasingh recalled an earlier starting point for *Intimacies,* a conversation in a seminar she had attended on questions of cultural migration.

"It was a very positive seminar on the whole, everyone saying how wonderful it was to be enriched by the process of migration. There was one Indian woman from the States, who was trained as a classical musician. She said that sometimes she finds herself in concert situations where everyone knows and appreciates the rules of the music – there's a kind of organic connection, an easy consensus. And when that happened, she felt a pang of... sadness. Not quite sadness, but a flash of self-recognition – that she had room for this classical purity while also being part of a more complex impure world."

So for Jeyasingh, being 'on the edge' suggested a doubled quality, the excitement of irreconcilable elements and the possibilities of exploring the space between them, as alluded to by the words 'third order' in the title. She likened it to travelling: leavetaking as a moment of departure as well as an excitement for the unknown. On a general level, this doubling, pointing in two directions at once, parallels her own move from the securities of classical dance towards the uncharted possibilities of contemporary movement.

First rehearsals

When starting rehearsals for *Intimacies,* however, Jeyasingh didn't elucidate these ideas straight away. "I don't think I'd do that, not in the very first rehearsal anyway. Sometimes if you pin things down at the beginning you lose the opportunities to hear other possibilities, because then the dancers will have something very fixed in their heads. I think when you rehearse you're hoping that something will emerge, and usually these things emerge by accident. And often I myself actually don't know what I'm aiming for at that stage. So I think you try and set goals that are not ends in themselves, but facilitating tasks."

She also finds the first rehearsal "very very difficult, because whatever piece you did before is somehow washing around in your consciousness." So instead of focusing straight onto these ideas, she uses 'diversionary activities' – what she describes as "a kind of scribbling in the margins".

"I always have particular movement ideas that I want to try out, which have nothing to do with any particular piece. They're just there all the time because they're always useful. A bit like if you want to make a garment: you're not sure how the cut is going to be, but practising your sewing is always going to be useful. It's like the basic raw material."

She gives an example: "Well, you can look at a Bharata Natyam adavu [a set sequence of moves] in terms of the physical rules it obeys, rather than in terms of what it is trying to achieve. So one adavu might be a collection of a spinal twist, a change of level, plus footwork accompanied by change of hand gesture. So if I just take that blueprint, how many other variations can one call up? That's just the kind of question that interests me all the time.

"So usually at the beginning I do those kind of things. It gives you some spare time – and keeps the dancers busy," she laughs, but adds that "it also sets other things in motion which actually take much longer to appear."

In addition to this choreographic doodling, she set up scenarios for improvisation. "For *Intimacies* I asked the dancers to think about leavetaking. One of the themes about the border, life in the borders, was this constant hello/goodbye way of living. Sometimes you are saying hello and goodbye at the same time. And saying goodbye is quite particular, because it's not sadness:

you say goodbye with, I don't know ... excitement. So I asked the dancers to choreograph on themselves, or with others, scenarios where they had changed in that way, from their own experience."

She also set up workshops around the theme of personal relationships, relationships with men, as another way of getting to the personal. "I was quite interested in how much the dancers were willing to give of themselves to these stories. And actually I realised very quickly that because they were classical dancers, even when they were talking about the personal, all that impersonal classical training was like a wall in front of them. I realised that if I wanted to get any juice out of them I had to really challenge them physically. It wasn't going to come out of them naturally, there was too much training between them and the source of their emotion."

Physically, then, she tried to unsettle the centredness, the certainty that comes with classical training. "I felt the key in some ways lay in dislodging all that smugness of the body – the straight back and fixed hips, all that containment. It's not as if in real life the dancers are contained in that way, but as soon as it was a dance situation in the studio..."

The movement generated from these sessions often didn't end up as part of the final piece; but they did affect its flavour, as Jeyasingh explains. "I think that's why hips and backs became a feature in *Intimacies*. There was much more displacing of the hip, the straight back. It made the dancers dislodge that classical centredness so much that without them realising it they were abandoning themselves to something – not directly to emotion, but to movement. But when you abandon yourself to movement you abandon yourself to emotion, you can't help it."

Composition

The material that emerges from the early rehearsals needs to be worked into shape. "It's not that difficult to generate movement – it's interesting, and the dancers enjoy it. But finally you have a whole lot of things and you think, well what I am going to do with it next? It's that compositional element which is for me the real choreographic challenge. Sometimes I find that I put off that stage for as long as I can because for me that's the hardest work."

The process is a constant dialogue with herself and the dancers. "I try things out at home, and often I can't do what I want, but I get an idea of the mechanics. So usually in a rehearsal I would go through these ideas, and as the dancers are doing it I would get more ideas about how it could be composed. It's like you work out the alphabet and the words, and sometimes bits of sentences, and as you're working with the dancers you find out what the sentences are, and they become little paragraphs.

"You have to find a form for the movement to inhabit, otherwise you just get people doing interesting movement. You have a feeling – like, yes, that would make a good beginning, or that section is good but it won't work at the end or the beginning. The process is purely one of personal judgement, your instinct as to what works and what doesn't. You can't plan it in a very logical way. I find that actually quite maddening, because I like to have everything rather tidy – I'm not the kind of choreographer who feels comfortable going into a studio and only letting chance and good fortune play their parts. But in choreography there are so many elements which are out of your control, like the dancers and how they do the movement, that you have to be partly an opportunist."

One example she gives with *Intimacies* was working for the first time with a dancer whose initial training was in ballet, Shamita Ray. 'I realised there was a kind of cultural divide to do with the centre of gravity: working with the weight going down or going up. With Shamita it was always going up, and at the beginning that made it terribly frustrating. She could do the movement, but because her weight was never down it didn't matter what her extremities did, there was something in the centre which was not what I wanted. And I suppose I had to find a way of accepting that some movements were going to be... translated, and I began to find that quite fascinating. And I think Shamita, with skills in two different styles, in some ways also exemplified the hybrid quality that I was trying to express anyway. Other dancers have different skills too, but they were brought together by that question of weight. With *Intimacies* that circle had to get bigger in order to embrace Shamita.'

Jeyasingh is an abstract choreographer, so the composition isn't ordered by narrative development. What kind of structures did she put in to shape *Intimacies?* "In any particular piece I think one is always trying to reveal the rules of the movement. It's an incredible challenge for the audience, like asking them to a reading of Chinese poetry when they don't know Chinese: they've got to understand the rules of the grammar and find out how the language works, and also then appreciate how you've broken the rules. The whole process, which in language takes years, with an abstract dance piece you're asking someone to do in half an hour. I think that's one of the measures of the success of the choreography: whether you get over the grammar."

Whereas in previous pieces that 'grammar' was often closer to the surface, more immediately recognisable in large patterns of movement, *Intimacies* is looser, more intuitively structured. "I suppose in some ways the pattern was in a different area – communicating an emotional meaning rather than, say, structural concerns. Or that the structural concerns in *Intimacies* were much more within the bodies of the dancers than with larger patterns. Most of my energy in *Intimacies* went into composing the body, whereas in other pieces I was more content to leave the body relatively unquestioned – I didn't ask people to displace hips and so on. *Intimacies* became much more an exploration of that, and I think the dancers felt a huge difference in themselves: the dance seemed to have shifted on to them, and it really communicated something about them, as women and as people."

Intimacies does, however, have an overarching, if somewhat diffuse level of large structure, moving from a jumble of activity at the beginning, through a gradual sharpening of focus on to individual dancers, the piece ending with a series of six solos. 'At the beginning of the piece we had phrases that were used later in the dance, but everyone was doing it at once, in a loose, anarchic way. There was a lot of detail in the phrases, but I wanted to show everything en masse, and then hopefully the eye would be attuned by the end of the piece, and able to look at the movement on a single body, because it needed all that focus and attention. But I didn't want to give all that at the beginning."

In order to attune the eye, Jeyasingh used a great deal of repetition. "Lots of repetition," she emphasises, "more than I would normally use. You'd see the same phrase, but sometimes in a very chaotic way, other times as part of a duet. Or the tempo would be different, or it would be placed differently, on the edge of the stage or with a different facing. Then by the ending you'd finally see the phrase in its fullest form, just done by one dancer."

Music

The choreographic composition developed alongside the musical composition, a commissioned score by Michael Gordon. "We didn't have any music when we started – I think I had a first sketch, which lasted about a minute and a half, within the first two weeks. Ideally with music you need some sort of sketch in your head when you go into the studio. But we didn't get a near-finished score until about five weeks into rehearsal. I'd made certain chunks of movement, and as the music came in I'd think, will this work with that? Sometimes it did, sometimes it didn't."

Usually Jeyasingh has quite a lot of input with the score, "but with *Intimacies* because Michael lives in New York I didn't really get to know him in a way that I would if he'd been more accessible. So there was lots of changing. Beginnings became ends and ends became middle, chunks were taken off – and it was all done through couriers. We did talk about the idea of leavetaking, and he used a quote from Purcell, the last aria from *Dido and Aeneas*. But apart from that quote, the music wasn't particularly emotional – not at all, in fact. And the first bit he sent me turned out to be unlike everything else in the music – very rhythmic, beat-orientated, quite hard – so I had a completely different idea of how the music would sound when I started."

Often a composer will supply Jeyasingh with some kind of score, a map which gives her a lot of structural information to work with. "But Michael said he didn't really compose like that, and it forced me to work in a different way. Also, with this music, you don't get any joy by trying to count it, it's more of a physical experience. So I cued into the dynamics more, letting the dance and music run in parallel lines. For example, in the last section, with the solos, the music has a little motif which hinges on a very asymmetrical use of rhythm. And the movement came from that motif, but it wasn't "sitting" in the music: sometimes it was delayed, sometimes faster.

"So the response to the music was very varied, and more to its effect than its structure. And often I decided not to parallel that effect – the first five minutes was very slow and sustained but I put very fast movement to it, movement that came from another section in the dance. In a way that relates to that tension of going in two different directions at the same time. Which I think I finally realised is what I wanted to communicate: that to-ing and fro-ing. It's not something that I thought of just last year, it's been with me ever since I did *Raid* [1994]. But each year one gets slightly better – hopefully! – at communicating these things.'

Responses

But Jeyasingh recognises that the communication in dance is a complex process. "I think with dance you can't get very particular ideas across, unless you have a story. Often in meet-the-choreographer sessions people will ask, what did you want to say? And I say we have to make the meaning together, there isn't something objective I have in mind that you have to get for the piece to succeed. Also I find that the meaning emerges, even for me, during the tour. The dancers and the musicians and the audience make the meaning together, and it changes. I may make changes myself, but even without changes the dancers possess and own the dance in a completely different way. And the way it communicates in Manchester might be very different from in the Queen Elizabeth Hall. So the meanings are very fluid, they don't exist anywhere apart from in that space between the stage and the viewer's eye."

Does this mean that she's happy with whatever the viewer makes of it, or does there come a point when she feels the piece is misrepresented? "What I sometimes find frustrating is the kind of agenda that gets in the way for that dialogue even to take place – when people come in with cultural presumptions about what I should or shouldn't be doing, or seeing it solely in terms of the bigger agenda of transforming Indian culture: either I'm being too Indian or not Indian enough. All of these are red herrings, very little to do with the dance piece. I think if people could sometimes neutralise these perceptions, they would realise they're very minor things that they're making terribly major. Like hand gestures. Sometimes that in itself signals "Indian Classical Dance" and then people think their responses have to be ordered by that fact without using their intelligence to ask: is the hand gesture important to this piece or not? They haven't even gone to that level, and history and custom and habit have already got them in a byway.

"So it was fine when one critic, who's usually liked what I've done, didn't like *Intimacies* – it was for compositional reasons, which is perfectly acceptable.

But with another, the whole review was about how my "ethnic source" had become unrecognisable, how I was setting thrusting modern values against "old world mystique", and commenting that there weren't any Indians in the audience. As if I had a duty to communicate some kind of recognisable Indianness – which I find outrageous: I have a duty to communicate dance. I'd worked on aspects of the dance, and composition, vocabulary, and all that didn't seem to stand for anything, it wasn't even mentioned.

"It happens less now, but underneath I think is a blindness to the fact that there is a contemporary Indianness. There is something basically wrong with the idea that to be Indian one has to be traditional – but it's so endemic within the thought processes of Europe that I think very intelligent people hold it without questioning its ludicrousness. It's one of the things that stops people from looking at what we do as a company."

Just as Jeyasingh uses facilitating tasks in rehearsals rather than trying to achieve set goals, so she sees her work with the company as open-ended. "I feel that my tryst, if you like, is with the future. So probably in twenty years' time I'll have a better idea of what responses I valued, what it all adds up to. I think my main interest is about questioning, I don't have any answers at all. I'm not even trying to make a Shobana Jeyasingh dance vocabulary, I'd like to think I make Shobana Jeyasingh dance questions. The responses to questions are always more subtle and more complicated than responses to answers. That's part and parcel of what the company is about."

Rosemary Lee

in conversation with Sue MacLennan

Rosemary Lee In Conversation with Sue MacLennan July 1998

Sue: *Rosemary, we are going to talk about your piece, Treading the Night Plain which you made for Ricochet Dance Company in 1996. What was the stimulus for the ideas for this piece?*

Rosemary: Well The main stimulus was the company itself, the fact that it was Ricochet commissioning me. I was invited to see Russell Maliphant's and Wayne McGregor's pieces. I was thinking, "what am I seeing and what am I not seeing in the company?" I was struck by how beautiful they were physically and by their movement quality, and how very professional and accomplished they were. So I started to think about what I would want to bring out that I didn't see in that programme. I wanted to try and bring out more individuality in each of them as performers; so singling them, finding their individual qualities that I could bring out and I wanted to costume them in absolutely the best way for each of them because again it looked like they were costumed as a sort of group. So I wanted to work with costume and with movement, and also to make them travel a lot, because I felt they had so much power and flow. I think those were probably my primary concerns, bringing out the potential in them, more individuality, and a very particular kind of energy, more rushing, more throwaway, not quite so considered and technical. Also, I was very drawn to the music of Terry Riley, early on, and listened to all his work and that was a key stimulus for the work.

Sue: *And do you always have the music before you start rehearsing?*

Rosemary: No, in the last works I have made like *Silver* with the Balanescu Quartet, the music gradually developed as the piece developed. So no, but I have to say if I'm in a mood where I want to be safe and feel secure, I love having the score first.

Sue: *So for the Ricochet piece, did you have a very particular or very generalised picture in your head before you started?*

Rosemary: Well once the music came I can't quite remember how this worked. I did a week at Middlesex University in the summer as a research period before I worked with them for six weeks in December. I got to know them and gave them lots of tasks that I would give in any of my workshops, using improvisation and lots of image based work, and they were very responsive. The music comes from *Cadenza on the Night* Plain for the Kronos

Quartet and the pieces are 'Diary of an Interplanetary Dream Collector' and 'Waltz of the Mythic Bird'. There is something incredibly expansive about the space the music evokes. So I started to get visions of a night sky which is difficult to put into words - constellations and stars, flying stars and shooting stars, galaxies, infinity and then other associations. Souls and Greek gods and god of the sky and dark imagery that's a bit transcendent and very airy; all of that was in the music for me. I wanted to make them into Gods in a way - kind of character Gods.

Sue: *So, were you given parameters to start off with, for example the number of dancers for the piece?*

Rosemary: It was intended to share the evening with another piece, so it was going to be around 35 minutes long I think. And I wanted to work with the whole company, two men and three women.

Sue: *But there wasn't money to commission music?*

Rosemary: No, just money for costumes and lighting, but no money for set.

Sue: *When did you choose the music?*

Rosemary: Do you know I can't remember! I could find out by looking at the videotape because I taped all the rehearsal process so I could look back at all those images. It feels as if I must have had it in the research week already, because of some of the images came from my thoughts on the music.

Sue: *Is that something you've done in other pieces - had a one week research and development workshop and then a big gap and then started making the piece?*

Rosemary: Yes, I did with *Silver,* a solo for Simon Whitehead. The making period was a bit stretched out but it gave us layers of imagery, different meanings and different ideas that then got intertwined, that you wouldn't perhaps get in a solid six week period. In that piece there is a part about his personal history and then images started to come up around horses and then we linked the two together. There is something about the ideas smouldering and digesting, and having time to look at books about horse movement and going to watch horses and having that time which you perhaps wouldn't give yourself in a single shorter period.

Sue: *Is it a way you like to work?*

Rosemary: Ideally I think it is. Not when I'm making work for myself necessarily, but for other people.

Sue: *And for Treading the Night Plain what other sort of research did you do beforehand?*

Rosemary: I looked through all my books on angels because I've got some interesting reference books as well as picture books. We looked at those together, at the different ways angels are depicted in different religions. I find the different theories of Heaven with the different angelic planes and orders - Kerubim and Seraphim etc - fascinating. There are also theories about different speeds of wing beats; the closer you get to God the faster they become, creating a huge light presumably representing God. Their wing beats are said to correspond to particular sound frequencies you can pick up in the universe. All very curious, and certainly food for thought for *Treading the Night Plain*.

Sue: *What was the outcome of the first week of rehearsal?*

Rosemary: I was left with motifs, I call them images, but I suppose they are sort of movement motifs that I really liked, that we were trying. I did quite a few tasks that we kept in the piece. So I was actually left with a patchwork of different bits of material that I would then structure in the six weeks. I was able to give myself enough time to construct, so I think the structuring of the piece is more elaborate than any other work I've made. During that exploring week they'd got used to the kinds of ways I was going to ask them to make material, so we actually had solo material already by the end of that week. I think we probably had their individual themes. For example, I did a lot of work in the first week with movement coming from the inside out, which is something to do with the message I might want to convey or an emotional content. They were great vehicles for making materials, but I wanted to go beyond that layer of making and inside them more, but physically, not just emotionally. We worked with visualisations of the spaces inside the body only manifesting in very minimal movement but with a clear visible inner intention in the dancers' presence.

Another task was to have a conversation between two body parts. Let's make the conversation between the sternum and the backs of the knees. And the backs of the knees want to go backwards in space and the sternum wants to go forwards. I wanted to make sure they didn't get too safe in any of the movements so this was a way of making them fall and be clumsy and to try to get the root of the physicality of the movement rather than 'let's make a pretty picture'.

I didn't want it to be cellophane wrapped, too polished, I needed to keep the inside there. So they'd be doing a conversation between sternum and backs of the knees and then the opposite, backs of the knees pushing forwards, sternum pulling back. I use that task a lot because it makes people break their habits. Then we went smaller and we said "imagine there's a little dot of light in your neck saying it wants the neck to go upwards spiralling and then there are two dots in your knees wanting the knees to shake". So you have two activities going on at the same time, but quite small and from the inside. And all of the dancers have their own internal pattern that worked for them, and that's in the piece. So for Steven it was his neck and his knees I think, and for Anna something in her ribcage and her neck. So I tried to look at the space inside the body, the space in the whole theatre, but also this whole element of space in the music being cosmic, a micro - macro kind of thing. So they imagined universes inside their bodies and travelled in the universes inside and outside.

Sue: *You've said a lot about moving through the space, so how do you get from that space inside the body to travelling through space?*

Rosemary: Very good question. On that first week again - it's funny how I remember making the material more than structuring it - I wanted to get again this business of not getting too safe and surface beautiful, to keep this rawness inside the energy, so you could see where things propelled from. I wanted them to cross the space backwards, so we improvised going back with different parts of the body leading it, something I do with children a lot, which they love. So it would go - elbow, back of the head, back of the knees, heel, hip - and they've got a sequence that I made up and they've got their own. But it has to be absolutely bolting through the space, so they are really dragged by those places, almost falling over, so you get this sort of feeling of jets of energy going through them backwards. I guess that's also to do with this cosmic thing of them being pulled by forces, pushing them through the space. Then there's a lot about them controlling or investigating, perhaps not controlling the space inside them.

Sue: *So a lot of it came from setting tasks or improvising as you have talked about with very specific instructions?*

Rosemary: Yes, like the business of them having the solos. Each is very literal and we started off with their names. They made solo material for each of the letters in their names, which again is a very straightforward thing that lots of people do, but its a way for me of getting quickly a first hand idea of how they create material. Usually it says something about them. We're not trying to shape the K of Kate, we're trying to get the essence of K. You know if Kate had chosen to do something very forceful there I'd see something about her drive, and if someone's more tentative I'd see another side of them.

We also used the image from their Zodiac sign. I worked with specific words linking to the theme, for example "shoot", "dart" and "explode/implode" - words that for me have this connotation of space.

Sue: *The things you've talked about are very much based on pure movement but linked to images of the cosmic, but you did say that characters started to develop from this investigation of the internal and the different links between different parts of the body, things about character. Do you want to say a bit more about that?*

Rosemary: Yes, characters did develop, although not in a kind of linear narrative at all. So when I saw Steve do his name, and then I saw him do this stirring in the neck and the swivelling in the knees, it occurred to me that he looked like a conjuror. I'm quite aware this is complete generalisation, but I have to go with first impressions. So he became a magical conjuring sort of figure and then I saw him a bit more like an alchemist who seems an archetype. I was trying to find archetypes for them so he was the alchemist and he was a bit the wise one, I felt. And then Dave had a fantastic sparkling quality, when I saw him move very quickly, a very smooth liquid movement but also very swift and nimble. So I kept with that mercurial notion and I saw him as a messenger or as a sort of Dickensian pickpocket. I could almost see line drawings of Dickensian characters in the sky or something, kind of odd constellations, Peter Pan-like. And then Karen has an incredibly buttery, smooth quality - unbelievable fluidity coming from the inside, and she seems very regal and has a real poise about her and so she became the queen for me, some kind of lost queen. Kate and Anna were more difficult to pin point. Kate seemed to have a birdlike quality, quite fluttery, almost a wounded bird at times, and birds were in there for all the dancers, a lot of it was about flight.

One of the other things we did was to work with elements of fire, earth, water and air, dancing with those elements. And we looked at which elements worked for them. Kate was incredibly comfortable in earth and she did these fantastic ploughing movements like furrowing the earth, and she's the plough and she leads the ship image through the space in the piece. She's not queenly but anchoring, and also a bit of a seeker. And Anna's much more mermaid-like to me. She's almost watery or under water and Anna and Kate have similar roles of being the eternal seekers. Anna is always looking up with her eyes and searching internally in her ribcage. She's the one that wants to fly most so she is often lifted.

Sue: *And did you talk to them about this?*

Rosemary: I hadn't planned to and this is where I broke my usual process in this piece. Dave particularly asked me a lot of questions, very pertinent questions. Usually I don't tell people what's in my head because I absolutely believe that if the work is right they'll discover it somehow. But here they wanted to know my process, so I ended up telling them a lot about what I was doing and I was very nervous about that. I think that sometimes consciousness can get in the way of the dancers' intuitive reading.

Sue: *But was it important to you that they understood the nature of the character you're developing for them?*

Rosemary: I don't feel I developed the character, I feel that it was almost like a picture rather than a development, so I didn't necessarily feel they would need to know. When I was dancing your work, I did not feel I had to ask you anything about the intention too much because I felt it in the movement, or I trusted I'd find the dance logic inherent in the complete work eventually. Some dancers need to know more earlier. I hopped the characters were embedded in the movement itself because of the intention and source of the movement.

Sue: *How about if there's a relationship between those different characters?*

Rosemary: Yes, we had to talk about that a lot and that's when gender issues came up, because there were two strong duets in the piece. One's between Dave, the messenger if you like, and the queen and the other's between the searcher and the alchemist, Anna and Steve. And we talked quite a bit about that relationship between Dave and Karen because it's as if he is protecting but also restricting her. She wants to escape and a lot of this is about being trapped on earth and wanting to fly; its a recurring theme that really comes a lot into my work, particularly my own solos. In **Treading the Night Plain** the women all want to fly and the men are in general more secure in where they are, they don't want the women to explore as much. This raised a lot of questions.

There's lot of counterbalance with the woman wanting to fly and the man holding her like the end of a kite. She's leaning out and he's catching her around the hips and her arms are beating and she's falling and he catches her again and she leans out over great heights. He's always supporting her or leaping around her like the messenger, almost servant-like quality but very loyal and protective. With Steve and Anna, there's a lot of riding each other. He stands on her and she is a bit like those flying figureheads on a ship, her back is arched and she's always flying. He stands on her back and holds her arms as if he's flying through the air on some mythic bird.

Sue: *And what were the questions about?*

Rosemary: Well particularly the supportive thing that the men were supporting the women in lifts. In *Egg Dances* I had been concerned to use the men and women equally in lifting material, and in this piece I choose not to. I just felt that these three women are like these sirens, they're so beautiful, and I wanted to exploit that. This trio of women had all this quiet power - the piece did become gender based and I meant it to be.

Sue: *But you managed to convince Dave...*

Rosemary: I told him it was intentional and... oh he was fantastic. When he saw himself as a rescuer and helper it was easier for him. He's stopping her, not because he's a strong man holding her but because he wants to stop her from flying or dying. Its almost as if there's something about dying too. That must be because of the night and space, and something about exploring unknown territory.

Sue: *So although we've talked about these characters and the relationships, you said a moment ago it was more of a picture. But I think the way we're talking about it it sounds quite narrative based in a way...*

Rosemary: There are narrative areas in the piece like the duets, or particular relationships that repeat. However, I wouldn't say there was a linear progression. I see it as these sky gods/characters interweaving in this vast space but not clearly reaching another destination by the end. They are swept around by unknown forces and resist or go with these but there are changes through the piece as the music takes them on a kind of journey of course.

I use the first piece to establish them as individuals within a group. They start with just their backs and their shoulder blades moving and the light fluttering and their breath affecting their rib cage. Ad then it expands out and you see the image of the women wanting to fly right from the start and then those duets start. Jon Lever made extra sound with actual bird wings and booming noises to link the two Riley pieces. During this Steve tries to assist them all as they leap from stillness. But they jump from nowhere and he catches them at the height of their jump. We call them 'sternum jumps' because the sternum leads up into flight.

The second half is much more about them all exploring space together, the rushing energy and the shooting through space material. There are skimmy, skippy phrases and three episodes set through improvising on intricate spatial patterns as a group. The bird-like images reccur and the ending is of orbiting lifts with the women in broken falling shapes above the men and Karen alone with her own internal pattern.

Sue: *So it is not narrative but more imagistic. Perhaps you're talking about a creation of an atmosphere?*

Rosemary: Definitely, which comes very much from the sound and what I saw and felt. At the beginning the theatre is very atmospheric. There's a feeling of them being lost in space, there is a feeling of there being a huge unknown that they're exploring, and they're travellers but they can't always govern where they go. You could think of them as souls or you could think of them as strange archetypal characters wandering through space together, a migratory group of refugees in space. I wanted to get a sense of lostness, vastness; sometimes they appear very vulnerable and small so I was very clear about the way they used space. I want them right on the edge; if they've got a solo in the corner or a duet I want it right in the corner or right at the back, not into where I call no-man's land, those halfway places between the centre and the edge. They had to give me a sense that the space they were inhabiting was way beyond the wings, and then other times when they were very powerful they needed to eat the space up.

Sue: *Were there particular things about working with this group of dancers?*

Rosemary: Yes, I was able to ask for more physicality, more articulation and more risk taking. I could challenge them physically more than I would with other people with different levels of experience. We have talked about these images that I had and the different layers because its not just one image - Dickensian pickpocket is totally different to a lost soul in space. In a way that's probably one of the most demanding things about the piece; it was hard for them a) physically, as it's an absolute killer, stamina-wise its difficult because of all the rushing and b) emotionally because as a performer the multi-layering of images must be quite difficult, there's lot of levels of being. I tried to explain to them that if they always focused on the intention of the movement, if they really went backwards through their elbow, through their neck, if they really felt falling, if they really were leaning and flying, it should work. So that's what I really wanted them to do, to stay with the intention, the inside, and not to wrap and package it on the surface.

Sue: *So does it work equally if they think "I'm being pulled back by my elbow" or "I'm a messenger"?*

Rosemary: Ah, what a good question. I think it works equally with the elbow being pulled back because those images for me and the characters are inherent in the movement material I saw Dave doing. I should say that I think the Dickensian characters are secondary to the spatial universal images. Those are stronger for me than the pickpocket thought that gave me costume ideas and developed material.

Sue: *The fact is that you didn't want to pin it down to the audience saying "I see a little Dickensian pickpocket running backwards through the street". You wanted a kind of resonance.*

Rosemary: Exactly. Thank you Sue, a resonance of it. The character helped to make his movement motifs more concrete so when we rehearse I might say "Do you remember it's a pickpocket that you remind me of, an ariel, so go quicker, cut that corner, look this way, don't smooth it..."

Sue: *Yes, so it's intriguing this.... its very movement based but it seems these images inform and help you to keep consistent patterning, the speeds, the angles and the dynamics of it.*

Rosemary: Yes, the quality and intention of the actual movements. Right. So, for example, the movement for Anna is something in her rib cage moving around and undulating, her eye is looking up to the ceiling. If she is searching in her ribs and her eyes are really looking and searching, then the movement will be right - in other words the movement will express my intention in a greater sense.

Sue: *Are there are other points of interest you want to mention?*

Rosemary: Yes, you've just reminded me that I made a conscious decision half way through the process, that I would use material I'd used in other pieces. I thought it hasn't been seen by many people, my work rarely tours widely, I love those images, so a lot of images came from the piece I made with students from de Montfort University, a whole duet and images of flying, holding, counterbalancing - all came from that piece. Some things from *Egg Dances* came out again so I actually consciously thought well let's find the images that were strongest and re-invent them.

Sue: *A lot of people do that without noticing or without acknowledging it. You look back and realise you've made the same piece over again in different ways.*

Rosemary: Yes, definitely, and I'm feeling better about doing that.

Sue: *I think we've got a really strong picture of the content and how you arrived at it. How did you approach structuring the piece?*

Rosemary: Isn't it funny, it's what I can't remember.

Sue: *Did you, for example, work in broad brushstrokes? Do you put big chunks together and then go back and refine them to get an idea of potential structure?*

Rosemary: Yes, this time I did. I've never done that before but I set myself a task and knew I had to finish it by a certain time. I'd got so much of the content. I then worked on the first piece of music from beginning to end I just worked on one section. I didn't chop around. I knew bits for the second section but not the order though I might have known the ending. I tried various beginnings and went through a lot of different improvisations. I'd give different orders, go away, look at the video, try a different order until finally something hit the music in the right way. I used the music structurally a lot and I think that's true for most of my work. Quite early on we established musical sections or recurring themes that related to each performer.

Sue: *There could be a stage that we've missed out here. We have the building and establishing of images and then you've organised these into sections and duets. And then the larger structuring is finding an order for those sections, and transitions presumably become very important?*

Rosemary: The dreaded transition! Like, what will work if they're doing that duet? Can the other duet exist in the space? Or where's Kate, is Kate doing her searching and when is her solo going to overlap? So, yes, I'm placing things and overlapping things and seeing what can read. It's quite a dense piece, but I wanted that because the music has that density. I wanted these things coming and going into the foreground, coming forwards and backwards overlapping each other, leaving a space, coming back again.

Sue: *So do you really analyse the music? Do you break down the structure? Did you have a score?*

Rosemary: I didn't have a score but I did get to know the music in great detail I don't get too analytical, but I'll say "Can you hear this theme where its going up? That's going to come back three times, can you hear it?" Yes, they are dancing absolutely to the music but it's following the line of the melody rather than counting it. The contours of it - it is more a landscape or a flow. The flow of the violin going through there, that they're following and relating to rhythmically at the same time. But its like going on a journey together with music.

Sue: *Tell us about your use of chance.*

Rosemary: I have the whole palette where I write the names of the sections, eg "Leighton Buzzard", the plough, episodes, the galleon. I cut them into separate pieces of paper and lay them out, put my hands over them and pick one out without looking; I'll look at it and write out the order that I get. Now I don't just accept one or the other, I'll just twist this, or think "Yes that would really work what a great idea", or I'll think "No I don't want to start with that I'm going to try again." So I try it again and I keep getting it and if I keep getting something I think something's happening here, someone's telling me something, so I'll reconsider and try it out. So it's a bit of manipulating but it starts me off, gives me a framework that I might leave, but I do think I use chance in almost every piece. I always think it is cheating though.

Sue: *But we have the whole precedent of Cunningham and chance!*

Rosemary: I know. Its something to do with using it when I get stuck, and then I think I'm failing because I've got stuck and I haven't found the structure myself. I go and do it, and come out and there's my structure and I come in with my massive sheet the next day with holes and things that might not work, but it does give the most fantastic framework to work with.

Sue: *I'm just surprised that you feel that its cheating.*

Rosemary: Because I think I should have been able to think it up.

Sue: *But its very similar to just writing your work out like that and then choosing different orders and selecting your favourite possibility... Because you're just doing it by chance and then making choices and manipulating it..*

Rosemary: Yes, that's true and may be its a way of getting consciousness out of the way if you think its a block. Which I do often think it is. I know my yoga teacher says "Take your brain away from your forehead", it takes away conscious stuff that gets in the way of your body when it is working instinctively. And I know I do that when I teach and when I do improvisations so may be I have to do it in the creative process as well sometimes.

Sue: *This piece had a very definite signature and it's interesting that you didn't use that traditional kind of process of making or teaching material for the dancers at all, but you still very specifically draw out very specific images and qualities.*

Rosemary: I know people have said it's a very Rosie Lee piece because of the images, the wings and the angel. Maybe I'm denying the fact that I actually do teach movement, not sequences of steps. I mean I must have taught them that whole duet. It's just that I'm not getting up and dancing a phrase. There are sections that I definitely choreographed in the more traditional sense and there are sections that I directed.

Sue: *I'm just trying to clarify the amount of work and personal hands on-ness that you have in forming this piece...*

Rosemary: I'm sure there's a huge amount.

Sue: *...That if people who are reading this have only worked with direct teaching of material or as that being the basis, so that they understand it's come from you as your own signature very clearly on it. Even though you're drawing different material from the dancers and they're contributing.*

Rosemary: Yes, I am actually very specific and want the dancers to experience exactly what I am after. I'm specific particularly about intention, quality and timing. The tasks I give that remain in the piece are selected to reveal a very specific quality I am after. For example, there is a sudden fall through the body underneath Karen's hand. I am not saying "Twist your knees to the right, put your hand..."; I am saying, "No, show me the plumbline falling straight through your body", and I'll get up and try to find that authenticity with them.

Sue: *Do you feel like you have a range of personal processes that you know can work?*

Rosemary: Yes, I do and I think a lot of them are in this piece actually. In a way it felt like the end of a period where I resolved a lot of processes, a lot of material images that I've used before and I didn't know where to go after it. Here it was, but with quite different dancers and perhaps it manifested itself differently but as you say, it's got that signature and it feels like it may be the end of some of those images. So now I'm having this year of research and development which is quite scary.

Sue: *I think it is very interesting and important to find the balance between accepting this body of things that you know can work, and merely relying on a process. I don't think we need to just drop those things we know we're good at and dive into the unknown just for the sake of it.*

Rosemary: No we don't expect or want that of other people, it's funny that we think we need to do it. These days I do feel more able to stand my ground amidst constantly changing fashions and trends.

1

Wayne McGregor
in conversation with Jo Butterworth

Wayne McGregor in conversation with
Jo Butterworth
June 1998

Jo: *The Millenarium was made after a 6 month research and development period and with a new company. Would you say, therefore, that it was essentially typical of your previous work or do you see it as a new beginning?*

Wayne: I don't really see it as typical because I think about my working process all the time, so I never have a sense of completeness. The beginning and ends of a piece have a longer continuum than that. It was different from a physical standpoint as I was starting with completely different dancers. And I had a different intellectual standpoint and range of interests after my intensive period of R & D. I had come up with very different questions from those I'd started with. So I entered the studio in a different way.

Jo: *How did you actually spend your time in the R & D period?*

Wayne: Well, I did a range of activity centred on questions about the relationship between dance and new technological developments. How was technology impacting on the possibilities of creating and performing dance? How could technology mediate ways of structuring content? Also, because I was working with new dancers from completely different training backgrounds, I simply wanted to spend time in the studio exploring their bharata natyam or ballet or different contemporary backgrounds. This enabled me to push the physical vocabulary and learn from the various training methods; and that really informed my decisions about who I would employ in the next project - what the physical body type might be like, what their range might be. I could then go out and actively search for those things in audition.

Jo: *So in hindsight, what were the major starting points of the choreography?*

Wayne: The idea for *The Millenarium* came from a cross between millennium and aquarium, a bastardised fusion of a word. I wanted to create a virtual space which wasn't bound by gravity but had this watery feel, and yet, at the same time, was a viewed space. It was actually a space which people could see into, like an aquarium. That was the starting point, but I also wanted to see how I could work with the aesthetics of the technologically driven environment.

So I wasn't using the technology like a shopping list, saying; "OK, the technology does this and I want to make a piece using that." I was attempting to work with a more digital aesthetic, to recreate an environment, an ecology of space, which worked with the idea of a degenerating or electronic image, but with a physical reality in a live space. I was interested in how I could work with a physical vocabulary which, in some way, jumped from a very naturalistic movement vocabulary to almost computer generated, cyborg-like movements. So those ideas were very much there at the beginning of the rehearsal process. Is that clear, do you think?

Jo: *Yes, but it's interesting that you say how __we__ wanted to continue. Are you including here your dancers?*

Wayne: Yes, it was a negotiated process. As I've become more confident in making choreography I've learned to value dialogue; it provides the possibility for change and empowers dancers to really take on board material and its meaning. It also provides me with more of a range.

Jo: *Do you then identify the stages of the choreographic process before you start?*

Wayne: Yes, I do. Typically I start by generating content and don't really think about structure in the early stages, say for the first five or six weeks. I'm looking at the language I want to develop to express some of these ideas. Obviously in the generation of content you do start to build in inherent structures and often I make a phrase which becomes a solo and the structure is almost pre-determined from the ways in which we made it in the first place. And often the content gives me a very clear rhythmic or structural direction but I try to remove my thinking from those things find the language first. What is the body doing and how is it doing it? For **The Millenarium** I was working at a notion of extremity; how far could I push the body? How could I make a disfunctional movement vocabulary look at certain times very fluid? How could I make it ricochet through the body and what were those movement pathways? How could we make that disfunctional movement really live? Could I generate a hybrid form of naturalistic, ie humanistic, almost gestural movement, and very digital movement? By digital, I mean movement that seems to blip through the body, is almost sampled, very rapid fire. And then there are moments of very organic movement which feels quite animalistic. I am searching to find that language through giving material directly to the dancers, working in improvisation, always based around an idea.

So I never do open improvisations. I always come in with a specific starting point. I choose a starting point which has something to do with the overall idea so it has some very specific link to the meaning of the piece, or its questions. That stimulus might be some text, it might be something more kinetic, like a video or something which is very alive technologically. It might be more conceptual. For example, one of the improvisations was about this disconnection between the brain and the body, thinking about the body as a container for space and replacing organs in the body with different organs. If we had a choice about which organs we would replace, what would our order of priority be? How could that create an architecture for improvisation? So the language became embedded with all these principles to do with technology. The technology isn't an adjunct nor is it just about structuring; it actually informs the choreography from the beginning. You see that it's a technological language rather than just a language which has been plonked into a technological environment.

I then start to see how that content can live in different ways. What would be the impact if, all of a sudden, some of that solo material was fused into a different sort of trio? What would happen if I took a solo and retrograded it or displaced it, or put the material on the floor? How could I then communicate something different with that solo ? How could I structure sentences which were very clear and quite extreme, but still make optimum use of the material? In this way I decided how the dancers could interpret the material and which dancers could give it a particularly interesting quality that I hadn't thought of. I then think structurally, and experiment with accumulative patterns, rhythmic and spatial structures. I spend weeks just trying material in a range of combinations and changing them, changing my mind, to either develop the content, or decide on the best structure for each particular idea. The content should continually resource the structure and vice versa, in a very lively dialogue.

Jo: *Inter-related?*

Wayne: Yes, really inter-related dialogue.

Jo: *And I can remember that at one stage you then had to deal with the other structural problem of how you, as a performer, became involved in this piece. You made a decision to make your own sections solo sections for a number of reasons I think.*

Wayne: Yes, I decided originally, that I wanted to integrate myself completely into the fabric of the choreography and be part of this whole environment. However it was also a reaction to the idea that the choreographer should only perform in the group sections of their own work. I kept thinking, oh yeah, I should be in the group sections, without really asking why? I was finding it difficult to generate the material objectively and be in there performing it honestly. Also I wanted to provide something that was special and unique to me. I could see the amazingly particular things the dancers brought, I knew what they were and I knew how I wanted to work with them. Yet I felt that I could probably tell a better story or offer a very different dimension if I provided a parallel journey to the group explorations. A solo body that offered a different dimension to the non-linear narrative of the piece, would give a very interesting tension between group and solo. Besides, it was easier to work technologically as a soloist without the other concerns about group material. I think that in *The Millenarium* some of the strongest relationships between the technology and the body are actually in solo form because then you really get the synthesis of both visual images. I had the opportunity to really make those connections and that's something I'm going to pull through to my next piece of work. How does that become more fluid throughout the whole piece? These questions influenced my decision to be separate, to provide myself with a journey which would give the audience a different dimension to the exploration of the theme.

Jo: *When were you able to start working with the other technological aspects of the piece? Because obviously at the very beginning of the rehearsal process those things weren't available to you, and then only some of them were available to you at the period of rehearsal in Birmingham.*

Wayne: That's what's frustrating about working with new technologies because normally, if you've got your dancers and a studio, you've got your raw materials. With *The Millenarium* we didn't have all the technological resources we'd envisaged at the beginning of the process. I desperately wanted to make sure that the technological elements were integrated from the very beginning of the piece but because the money came late, the technology became a distant collaborator. It was like having a composer in a different country and negotiating what the roles would be - and although that threw up very exciting challenges, it didn't provide enough integration into the whole piece.

So I used technological hardware as an external collaborator and that had a big effect on how we structured *The Millenarium*. I had to be clear about what the dance content was and how the visual components would work with a dance structure in a projected way. I had to decide in advance how that would work because we only had two weeks of technical time at that stage and couldn't really make massive changes. So the structure was determined earlier than ideal and was lead by the dance. I would have preferred to work with the two together to find new structure and new ways of presenting that material. That's a great learning curve. It pushed me to really focus back on the vocabulary in digital terms. How could I think about movement in negative space without actually providing a negative space? How could that movement vocabulary make perspective look different?

Jo: *So how many weeks did you actually spend working with the dancers without the set?*

Wayne: Eight weeks without the technological resources. I knew what the set was going to look like and I'd worked simultaneously with what the content of the images would be. It was just that direct relationship between body and image that we weren't able to connect with until two weeks before the opening.

Jo: *So two weeks before the opening you actually got part of the set?*

Wayne: Part of the set and part of the projection.

Jo: *And were there any changes that were made then based particularly on the exploration of those elements?*

Wayne: Yes, what I had visually from the projection material and from the slide images, from working with intelligent lights, the cyber lights etc. We'd worked on a range of visual content that we were only able to edit and structure much, much later. Because we had to put it on to video format, and not on laser-disk, the time delineation had to be structured much earlier and we weren't able to make last minute choices. So the content was there; what we then worked on was how that would interact with the established structure of the choreography. And that happened at the same time as the music was written for the piece, so although we'd talked about the possibilities of music - what the flavour, the palette of the music would be and how that sound ecology would work in the space, the generation of that material happened at a late stage because I wanted to make sure that the connection between the music and the graphic elements was very, very clear. So it wasn't a music and dance collaboration, it was a music/graphic and graphic/dance collaboration. And the whole ecology of the space then worked in a particular way.

Jo: *So during the eight week rehearsal period you didn't use the music that was subsequently utilised in the final piece?*

Wayne: No, I worked with sound ideas that I knew I wanted to develop later on in the score. I wanted the music to live in its own right and

I wanted the dancers to provide the rhythmic texture. This is often hard to get right in a very long piece. How could you have a quite dominant sound score, a score which was in some way very hypnotic and which lulled you into a false sense of what the sounds were, and at the same time have your dancers fighting against that with a rhythmic texture which was very different? What would that tension be? How long could we sustain that sort of energy and how did that work? The graphic element also provided an external rhythmic structure, so in this case it wasn't necessarily the music that always textured the rhythm but often the graphics and the kinetics of the movement together.

Jo: *And your music collaborators were cognisant of that?*

Wayne: Yes completely, and they worked a lot with creating what they called an "ecology of space". So it wasn't simply music for dance, it was very much about how we can create this notion of an environment with a life of its own.

Jo: *That takes us through the making of the work and perhaps to the first performance of the work. What happened then when you saw the work for the very first time? You felt it, you performed it, you saw parts of it and you got your first feedback when it was performed at The South Bank. What sorts of changes occurred after that stage?*

Wayne: For me there's always an intellectual change. I mean right up until the dress rehearsal I'm still very much on the outside looking in. In performance however I have to completely disassociate myself from the choreography and just be inside it. So for the first few weeks, certainly the first 10 performances or so, I was just getting used to my role, even though I've done all the choreographic preparation and lived with the ideas.

Jo: *But your role changes?*

Wayne: Yes, my role completely changes, so it takes time to sense how to make my journey real. And then because we've done a lot of performances, the dancers have not only had time to get involved in the vocabulary but I've also been able to stand outside things. It is difficult to decide whether to change material or let the work evolve. Its always a tension for me. In *The Millennarium* circumstances made me keep the piece as it was, even though I did have time after the opening to re-work it. One of the dancers had quite a severe knee injury so I already had to re-work the piece for 7 dancers. I didn't want to replace my lost dancer however, because that whole process of getting the material into your body is a really long one, its not a thing you can do in two weeks or something.

Jo: *Because it is a new vocabulary?*

Wayne: Yes, by the time we got our lost dancer back the piece had evolved
           and I wanted to save my energies and questions for the generation
           of the new piece even though that would be 12 months - 18 months
           later. I understood what decisions I'd made. Although I wasn't
           happy with all of them I felt that the piece should live in its own
           right and with only very minimal changes.

Jo: *So in hindsight now, looking back at the whole process of making
           and also having the opportunity to perform it so many times, what
           for you is the most stimulating thing about making and performing
           the work?*

Wayne: I think definitely working with that group of dancers. I took me a
           long time to choose that group of individuals, and the way in which
           we were able to negotiate a language between us really pushed my
           physical vocabulary into a different place. It has really liberated me
           in terms of thinking about what the body can do and where I can
           push the body in the future. And also, even though I wasn't
           completely happy about the technological interaction I am really
           aware that it was the beginning of a longer journey. This is the first
           piece in a series over the next three years. There are so many
           questions to research. The other major inspiration in *The
           Millennarium* has been the audience response, particularly in
           relation to the seventy-minute duration and the challenge of
           engaging people in that type of sound ecology for so long. The
           feedback told us that people had been really inspired and dialogue
           with the audience had been really important, even though it was not
           always completely positive and often very critical. But actually the
           actual engagement of talking about the issues and how the piece was
           working, provided me with another kick start.

Jo: *And for the dancers, what do you think has been the most
           stimulating moment for them?*

Wayne: I think they talk a lot about the performances because I think its
           unusual, now because of funding situations, to perform a piece
           enough times to really feel that you own a lot of the material. And
           we've had over 40 performances of this and they've had the
           opportunity to really submerge themselves in the choreography.
           And I think the language is quite a difficult language, its not a thing
           that you can acquire quickly.   And so the opportunity in
           performance to really go as far as they can go with this has been
           really, really challenging for them. They say to me that every time

they go on stage it doesn't feel that they've done 40 performances, it feels really new and they're still very nervous about it. I think it is because it is so complex and a lot of the responsibility really lies with them on the stage at that time.

Jo: *So what kind of focus do you think they bring to it when they go on stage? What is their new intention every time they enter the space? Are they dealing with the technical challenges of it or must they be dealing with more than that?*

Wayne: Yes, they're definitely dealing with the technical challenges, but the more they get used to it the more their muscle and movement memory increases their facility in the language that we've got and they become more comfortable. I've been very interested in making sure that the material doesn't look comfortable. I don't like material to look easy. I really like the awkwardness of extreme movement. For some choreographers the aspiration is for it to look very seamless and easy and workable in the body. I actually like the difficulty of it, the actual difficulty of the interpretation of it. The piece is essentially an abstract work; they don't have a narrative progression through the piece or a feeling of character, so its about continually finding something fresh in their interactions. How can they make their own sense of a duet and communicate this to an audience? Their focus also changes, because as performers we always bring our own personal energy of the day to a performance. Every performance is different, but in that difference you find something new and you take that through to the next one or you abandon other things. I think one of the things that we're all working on now is how to gain more emotional impact from the vocabulary. The language is so accomplished but its also very disassociated from emotion and yet we generate it from a very emotional base.

Jo: *You lose that?*

Wayne: Yes, the interpretation goes so far into abstraction that it becomes remote from the emotional base. How can we start to bring that back again so that you can see the root of the vocabulary? That's our focus now.

Jo: *Finally, you've talked briefly about the next work and your desire to maintain the company. What would you like to say about the next piece?*

Wayne: One of my concerns about making a trilogy, and why I took so long to choose the dancers, was that I wanted to work over a longer period and develop with the same group. So I'm keeping the same dancers, which is great, and we'll have a longer rehearsal period of around 15 weeks and the major difference is that we've got all the technology that we want from day one of rehearsals. So we'll work a lot with improvisational technologies, with digital film and projection and this whole notion of presence and absence straight away to generate content.

Lloyd Newson
in interview with Jo Butterworth

Lloyd Newson interviewed by Jo Butterworth
18 August 1998

Lloyd Newson studied psychology at the University of Melbourne where he also began his dancing career. After dancing with companies in Australia and New Zealand he came to Britain and gained a one year full scholarship to study at the London Contemporary Dance School before joining Extemporary Dance Theatre. By 1986 he had formed his own company DV8 Physical Theatre. The company aims to re-invest meaning in dance particularly where it has been lost through formalised techniques - pushing beyond the traditional and aesthetic inherent in most dance forms to enable a discussion of wider and more complex issues. When we spoke he had just returned from Copenhagen where he had been reworking his seminal piece *Enter Achilles* with new cast members.

I began by asking Newson about the points of departure for his choreography, about where the ideas, the intentions, the themes of his work come from. I was wondering whether they were essentially personal or political?

"I really don't see a difference between what is personal and what is political, and therefore I prefer to look at the individual's actions, responsibilities, and how they reflect on the large political, sociological, psychological arena. So in many ways I don't see a tight separation between those things. I think what most distinguishes the work of DV8 from a lot of other dance makers' works is that it is concerned with issues. It delves into how individuals relate to one another emotionally and intellectually, rather than being about movement patterns, design patterns, like moving human wallpaper. My work in fact to a large degree fights against uniformity, which traditionally has been used and seen as a dance strength. Of course, unison work, and having people of a similar size moving together can have a power about it, but it is the same kind of power that is also inherent in fascism".

For their next forthcoming project DV8 have advertised for women over 26 who do not necessarily conform to the traditional dance stereotype physically. "We have had 6 applications from women over 30. Only one is fat, none are old - and this is despite searching for body types outside the clichéd dance norm, yet when we open our audition to people younger than that we have 400-600 applicants. This raises questions for me about why these older women are not continuing in dance: how do they perceive their bodies, who are the people who reinforce notions of conformity - the schools, the critics, dance audiences - and what is considered acceptable in dance as a form? How do these attitudes affect people's psyches? It is my desire to challenge what is traditionally defined as dance, and who can do dance, and what dance can talk about. It feels like more than half the dance makers I've seen have never scrutinised or analysed the politics of the form they are employing.

"When I was with Extemporary, I was really upset when the company got rid of the older dancers to replace them with younger ones, because I felt that there was so much they had to offer. Perhaps they weren't yet offering it, but thepotential was there. And why is it that so many women dancers are not going on with dance? Maybe it just doesn't satisfy them when they become adults? Or perhaps after a certain period the ego orientation of dance, the beauty obsession, the dieting, the tricks - just feels empty. Perhaps the concerns of choreographers are not enough to stimulate them, they tire of being told what to do, with a form that has little real connection to the outside world. I think this is the tragedy of the form ...... how do we keep people interested?"

We discussed the current situation in the dance world, where much is still assumed about culture, training and intellectual rigour. For Newson, the very people who should be challenging the views of dance, pushing it forward, are not sufficiently aware of current thinking, for example in feminism, politics, social issues and gender studies. "We are talking about contemporary dance makers, are we not? Just to put people in baggy costumes does not make change, indeed it seems a very tokenistic move. I have even read critics who have lambasted female dancers on-stage in the last ten years for not shaving their armpits! Now that is an indication of the perpetuating circle of values."

It seems that Newson is particularly critical of the genre of modernist work: "After various associations with different dance schools in London I became aware that particular tastes were being imposed on their respective students. Their teaching was not about exploring a range of approaches or about nurturing individuals' development - moreover the institutions seemed to reduce dance's aesthetic and its concern to such a tiny little arena that I felt that they were choking individuality, and therefore dance's potential development as a form.

"It is blatantly obvious why people are not coming to contemporary dance - because it doesn't relate to their lives, full stop. It is not a big mystery. And not enough people are thinking about why dance is the ugly sister... because it is not thought through enough, it is not seen as intelligent enough, and it is often preoccupied by youth and beauty, and I am tired of that. I've always been tired of that - even before I turned 30!"

By contrast, some of the most interesting people who work with DV8 have generally done something else in their lives before they come to dance, like training in computers, ceramics or acting. Newson values the fact that they bring other significant life experience of the real world into dance. He finds frustrating the fact that "because people have got to train from such an early age, they don't have exposure to all sorts of other life experiences, and dance schools often become nothing more than cloning factories. The result is a product on stage that is a highly reduced reflection of life's concerns; people say "Oh, shouldn't dance be about beauty", but to be quite frank, beauty can be many different things. Having Diana Payne-Myers (a 70 year old woman) naked on stage in **Bound To Please** for me was infinitely more beautiful that seeing a gorgeous tall Swiss blond woman doing a perfect arabesque - because it is the context and meaning that makes something beautiful and touching. Beauty is the breadth of human experience - the struggle can also be beautiful. And so much of dance is to deny the struggle.

"If you can't do four pirouettes, you do two, if you can't do two, well look what else you can do. Not only is the current accepted aesthetic tightly defined, but it also constantly denies the notion of failure, and therefore half of our existence. And that's just the beginning. What about fat people, disabled people, older people?"

Newson has been invited to teach numerous international choreographic workshops both in the UK and abroad, and feels that his methods can engage both contemporary and classically trained dance makers: "Even when I work with a classical ballet dancer who works with abstraction, I can deal with that because my process is about making them question how they make work. 'Why are you doing that movement, what is its intention, what is its purpose? Essentially, what are you trying to say and communicate?' And it is not that I am necessarily against an arabesque per se, but you must know why you do it, you must think what an arabesque is, what are the politics of an arabesque; and I recognise that few dancers have ever been asked to question that.

" I think that is at the heart of DV8's dance making; every movement is questioned. As part of my research year I spent a week observing Mike Alfreds with his company, and I realised more and more that my work has become more analytical in terms of intention, focus, subtext, just like the way a theatre director breaks down text."

Research and Development

DV8 are known as a company who fight hard for funding to engage in research and development processes, and to gain periods of experimentation. I asked what the rationale was for this. "If you look around at a lot of the major companies, there is generally a plateau, a critical point around the twelve year mark. I saw it happen with LCDT, with Rambert, with Theatre de Complicité and Cheek by Jowl... Most people then fade or stop, because they feel that the pressures of running a company, to keep producing, are counter-productive to their creativity. Art initiative suffers if it is forced to operate like a factory floor. As we are talking about contemporary dance, we have to keep developing and changing. If you are under pressure, and everybody is subjected to and feels the pressures to make successful work, then there has to be a strategy for experimentation, which in turn is our only chance of rejuvenation. The climate has changed very much since the mid- eighties when we were first making work, when there was much more openness about experimentation, so I have come to the point where I can only really attempt risks and possible failures in my research period - that's where I really play with ideas. Without this I would be fearful to try new ideas and work with new people. So I invite new people to these research periods, I try and change my tactical approach, and I really do research....."

He gives an example: "When we were researching for *Bound To Please,* we were looking at people's experiences as dancers. Unfortunately a lot of people who worked with me then didn't really want to go back exploring ...they had left dance ....they didn't want to do arabesques any more... they didn't mind doing it in training but they didn't want to do arbitrary dance phrases on stage. This brought up a lot of major issues, largely to do with their value as people, when they were only (even though it was a theatrical device) seen as dancers.

"Before that though the research was about isolationism in the body - in *Bound To Please* we have a whole section where we just use heads, other sections where we just use arms, or the torso, looking at isolated parts of the body, rather than thinking --which so often happens with dancers -- that the whole body has to move in a fluid, connected manner. How can individual body parts speak? How can they be read? Connecting meaning to movement is what it is all about."

Another example came from their last research project looking at life in greasy spoon cafes, where he sent people out to cafés to observe behaviour, to see what information was conveyed through different people's body language and their interpersonal dynamics. When they returned to the studio they were asked to extrapolate what they had seen so that they could abstract it, and use the principles of the movement patterns that had been observed to make phrases. Though it is true that most dance is made in studios, Newson likened the dance studio to " a black hole, it is like a sacrosanct yet sterile environment that after a while feeds upon itself, and I suppose that last research period reflected my greater concern about dance trying to connect with and talk about the real world. So it seems logical to send the performers out to observe and interact with it."

The research and development period for *Enter Achilles* happened almost two years prior to the piece, suggesting that sometimes there can be quite a significant delay between ideas being initiated and the work that emerges a few years later. Sarah Hill of Dance Productions set up a five-week period in Glasgow, and Newson found himself struggling to investigate the distinction between subtleties of the spoken word, and trying to find the same subtleties in movement. The improvisations were quite frustrating and quite tough. Yet suddenly, he found a new direction for the experimentation: "One day I just went down to order a drink after we had finished rehearsals; we were all sitting around rather tired, and I noticed that everybody was drinking pints of beer - and that was the beginning of that - I said 'Let's bring pint glasses up to the studio tomorrow' - so by being open to what was around me - the pint glass became a metaphor for all sorts of things in the piece." It is obvious from the three examples cited above that the very different circumstances that come up in research periods lead to very different types of dance pieces. One of the challenges is about making or finding an appropriate vocabulary for each work. Another example from the Glasgow R and D period exemplifies: "For example - how do I talk about the situation when a policeman refused to hold the hand of a car accident victim because he might be seen to be homosexual? So I thought, how do I represent something like that physically - and I started talking to some of the heterosexual guys from my company, and they said "Oh, it's not a problem - we can make physical contact with other guys" - so I said "OK, walk hand in hand down Sauchiehall St", - they lasted three blocks - they couldn't bear the tension. So I questioned, how do I show this? When is it acceptable for men to hold hands - perhaps when they are doing aerial work? - so then I started investigating trapeze work. We brought in a rope worker to train our dancers because I needed this metaphor to talk about the issue of when it is acceptable for men to hold hands. So these two men holding on to a rope do this whole duet about holding hands and about maintaining physical contact, because if you don't, you die. But then when they get down on the ground, and they are still holding hands, one gets very nervous and anxious because there is no excuse, supposedly, to hold hands, and generally this behaviour is deemed unacceptable for two men."

In the company training, when DV8 make each new piece they bring in different people to develop new skills; in *My Body, Your Body* they did aerobics and long distance running to build up stamina, in *Strange Fish* Newson was very interested in the notion of being knotted up so they brought in a Yoga teacher, and voice teachers are brought in at times to work on sections that use text. People are brought in according to the subject matter. "When we were looking at football, why is it considered acceptable for men to do footwork around a football, but not to do footwork around Irish dancing or ballet? So we brought in an Irish dancing teacher because I wanted to explore the difference between those two forms - what is acceptable and unacceptable male movement?

"And I think that attitude suggests that we will do whatever we need to do. And if I can't find movement, I will also use words. I am not a purist -- I am not going to silence my breadth of expression or trade complex scenarios for purism. All I want to say as a fundamental principle is, make it clear and fight to be specific and detailed - however, through all this my interest is in conveying stories through movement."

The research and development periods are all videoed, all documented, broken down so that Newson can go back and refer to them in preparation for the actual piece. Much will be rejected and not used at all.

The rehearsal period

The form of the preparation for the actual rehearsal period does not follow one clear method, but is constructed around ideas synthesised from the previous period. For example, for *Enter Achilles,* Newson found five or six particular choices from the five week workshop that really gave him the spark and the momentum to continue - and these ideas were taken into the rehearsal period.

One exploratory idea was to take some pint glasses into the rehearsal; another was that "we should start experimenting with the idea of the men using one another as furniture; that we should look at fluids, play with the idea of men sharing fluids together and of intoxication, and the connotations of that. We looked at videos of documentary programmes on binge drinking in Wales on Friday and Saturday night and the violence that occurs after drinking 8 or 9 pints in one evening. And most importantly, we tried to look out at the world and our experiences of men amongst men, and to reflect this back in our work."

The notion that the dance work must exist in its socio-cultural context is a recurring theme for Newson. In order to keep him generating movement, and interested in dance, it has to have some personal resonance to his emotional and intellectual life. He is simply not interested in work that does not focus clearly on content. "I have done workshops with Twyla Tharp, Cunningham and Cage - just using mathematical formulae to make movement, using retrograde, inversion or random chance - while it is important - and I use those processes - in themselves, they are just a means to find, or structure material. So many people in dance are working with formulae alone, and no matter how intricate that is, to me it always feels vacuous and empty."

We discussed his choice of cast in terms of each new project. It is evident that he chooses people who are appropriate to the needs of the subject matter and with whom he can collaborate, people who can bring an openness of attitude and thoughtfulness to the process. "They have got to be interested in the subject matter - a couple of times I have chosen people who said they were and then when it got to the point they actually weren't interested or hadn't thought about the subject matter. I cast like a film director casts, according to what the script deals with, so for example there is no point in my looking at the relationship between an older woman and a younger man and trying to get one of my young female dancers to try and look like an older woman. That would be patronising, and also unbelievable. When we were doing *Enter Achilles*, I was very concerned to try and find guys who looked like regular guys in the street, not the white pasty long-limbed delicate waifs you often find in class.

"I wanted that random sample of eight men on stage. The trouble is, every time I start trying to find older, fatter men, they don't materialise at the audition; they are afraid to be on stage. When we made *MSM* about cottaging, I asked two things of those auditioning; they had to be prepared to be naked on the stage, and to go to places known for cottaging to feel the atmosphere, to know how tense it can be, or frightening, or funny, whatever. Interestingly enough, almost all of the men I was interested in casting decided no, because they were afraid to be naked on stage, afraid to have their penises seen by a large audience. Without that openness of mind and vulnerability, you know you would experience blocks in other areas. Incidentally, only one man finally ended up being naked in the piece - however, it was the principle that was relevant."

Since 1990, after DV8 had finished **Dead Dreams of Monochrome Men** and had made the film, Newson made a deliberate choice to leave behind that very intense, dark and exhausting physicality of his earlier pieces and decided to try to bring humour into his work. Challenged by a film maker making an international dance series, who assumed that dance could not deal with humour, "I decided to try and create more imagistic, humorous theatre, the traces of which can be first seen in **If Only**. I soon discovered that it was too frightening to go into a studio without a story and structure being pre-written. I couldn't do it any more, it was like going into a deep black hole - you need some structure - though you also need to be free to throw that structure out. So from then on, for all the pieces, **Strange Fish, Enter Achilles, Bound to Please**, I would write a scenario."

Becoming his own dramaturg and writing a loose structure before the construction period has also allowed the company to have sets built in advance, so that they could then live on the set and ensure that it was embodied as part of the performance. "It needs to be lived in, and you need to allow ....the body and the architecture to interact on stage.

"The script provides a guide in helping me structure the rehearsal period, both day to day and overall. For example in **Enter Achilles** we did a whole range of improvisations based on what is acceptable male physical contact, about what is considered an acceptable way for a man to walk, to talk. We played with the simple idea of straight and bent movements, how these affected how we felt and how they were perceived externally. We looked at the pressures on men to play particular sports, we'd talk about relationships with our fathers, our mothers, our best male friends, what we expect from them, and how that differs from our relationships with our female friends... and then we would have to get to specifics, because you can generalise and make all these theories but it's the specifics that are interesting. In the end, the interest lies not so much in how we do it, but in how he does it, and how specifics can often contradict theories, and are often very conflicting, and how that becomes human, complex and revealing.

"Generally I set up improvisations in rehearsal based around these concerns, so, if any improvisation occurs, it always has a direction and a focus. I've been in companies where they say -'oh, just improvise for a couple of hours', but about what? The aimlessness of that is so frustrating and mind-numbingly boring.

"Another way of working that I use that sometimes poses a problem for dancers, is that in order for really interesting deep material to come up, like analysis, you have to let go of your subconscious, and if somebody truly lets go in improvisation it is impossible for them to remember exactly what they did, because that is a conscious process. That is why we use a video camera. Many dancers however, don't know how to improvise. They don't know their own way of moving because they have often been rigidly trained to move in one way or style only.

"Obviously there are endless means of constructing the work - task setting, observation and translation, working directly from text; occasionally I even set steps! These methods combined with structured improvisation are my way of discovering new and appropriate dance content and of finding individual voices within the company, thus distinguishing how each of them moves differently, and how interesting and unique their differences are." Generally DV8's works are about seeing individuals on stage, therefore Newson tries to nurture their individual vocabulary, providing a focus, some boundaries for the improvisations and tasks. Company members appreciate the opportunity to combine their creative work with Newson's, and he sometimes takes part, but "generally I stand out because I have to be the 'eye' - and that is part of the reason why I stopped performing, because once we had over four people in our company I felt it was impossible to be on stage, and keep an eye on people's performance, so I removed myself, and now I sit through almost every performance our company ever does, giving notes and making changes... it never stops. For example, when *Bound To Please* first showed in this country, it was a totally different piece to what was presented in London three months later...That process is true of almost all of my work. Without constant change and development, a work becomes dead for performers and audience."

DV8 do a massive amount of touring each year, particularly in Europe but also in the States and beyond. The response to his work out of England is phenomenal, highly praised and appreciated. Yet Newson is concerned that this takes its toll on the performers and the company as a whole; and they are reliant on money from co-production in order to fund the British tour and subsidise the next necessary period of research. Reworking and touring a piece like *Enter Achilles* became necessary to ensure time to research the next project. This is the first time that DV8 has remounted a past work and it has become a particular challenge to the company's choreographic process.

"It has made me more aware of just how exactly every thought must have an intention, focus, beat, duration, change... how everything must be shaded to create a variance of emotional range... and it made me realise that yes, our work is like acting, you do need to apply all those things to do with craft, you need to be able to break down a movement as you would a text, so that it is clear, precise and exact. There are thirty different ways to pick up a glass, and each one says something different. Basically I try to impart that realisation to the people that I work with... and once they start knowing that, they can start to make contact with another person's arm and each gesture can say something different."

Because the work is devised with a particular group of people in the first instance, there can be some quite radical changes going on in changes of cast. New performers haven't been through all the intense research, and because the movement has come from someone who makes it unique to him, trying to get somebody else to do exactly the same doesn't work. Newson finds himself working with the qualities of the new individuals and adapting some things to suit them in order to sustain some truth.

"The other thing about dance making is that a lot of people I work with are really committed to new work, therefore they not interested in becoming a repertory company, and the only reason we are redoing *Enter Achilles* is to pay for the research this year. I mean, we've been offered to take it to both Broadway and the West End, but we don't want that because it would kill us, we want to keep making new work, we don't want to live a piece for ever. Our work is intricately linked to personal development and it is important not to get stuck in repetition and the values of commercialism."

Newson's role

Newson's role in the company is much more than that of a traditional choreographer, because the work is devised and collectively made. He sees himself as a stimulator, a facilitator, a teacher, but he also feels that equally he is learning a great deal from others. He recognises his responsibility to keep finding ways to open up every different person in the company, to maximise their performance potential, and yet he is also aware that whereas some are hungry to go forward, others need more support. "Some people are so surprised that they are capable of something, and often I have a greater belief in the person than they have in themselves. Most people are capable of producing incredible performances, but most people also carry blocks. Some are reluctant to go into new territory for many reasons. I can push, cajole, but at a certain point, unless they are prepared to let go of their psychological blocks, I can't do anything. The flip side of this is that DV8 have produced some exceptional performers who, prior to joining the company, hadn't maximised their potential."

Of course, that also means that DV8 might lose their most capable collaborators, but he is generously philosophical about that too: "I love it when the people I work with go off and make their own work, growing and taking responsibility. My understanding about the subconscious/conscious, the inside world/the outside world, is also applied to makers and instruments. I feel they should be interchangeable, and to be a balanced person I think you need to experience both. And to be quite truthful, many choreographers really do use their dancers like that, they just don't credit them, and that upsets me... one thing DV8 has always said is that the work is devised and collectively made..."

British Association of Choreographers

Founder Patron Sir Kenneth MacMillan
Patrons Robert Cohan CBE and Gillian Lynne CBE

Affiliated to Dance UK

The British Association of Choreographers acts as a platform for choreographers from all sectors of the dance world and is the only artist-led professional association for choreographers working in Britain.

We aim to

- Raise the profile of choreography in all media, to promote greater understanding of the craft/art amongst those outside the field of dance and to offer advice and support to all our members.

- To act as a pressure group in protecting the interests of our members and in gaining rightful recognition

- To provide opportunities through informal meetings at organised events and to promote the Choreographers Directory

- To offer mentoring, training workshops, master classes and observer schemes

- To respond to enquiries by our members and to educate the general public concerning the practice of choreography and issues pertinent to the profession of choreography.

For further information please contact
Fionna McPhee, 16 Durham Road, London N2 9DN
Telephone and Fax 0181 444 9437